HOTEL TO HOME

HOTEL TO HOME

INDUSTRIAL INTERIORS INSPIRED BY THE WORLD'S MOST ORIGINAL HOTELS

— *By Sophie Bush* —

Contents

Page 5

Introduction

Pages 6-69

Structural Features

Pages 70-145

Materials

Pages 146-205

Colour

Pages 206-267

Feature Furnishings

Pages 268-313

Lighting

Introduction

— *By Sophie Bush* —

FOUNDER | WAREHOUSE HOME

"THE WORLD IS A BOOK AND THOSE WHO DO NOT TRAVEL READ ONLY ONE PAGE"
AUGUSTINE OF HIPPO

When I travel, I hope to be inspired. Wherever I go, I try to stay in hotels with authentic stories and exceptional interiors. As an interior designer and a design writer, and not least as a homeowner, I am always looking for new ideas. The challenge faced by every hotel is to make each of its visitors, wherever they hail from, feel at home for as long as they stay. So hotels can serve as great sources of design inspiration. Over the years, I have discovered remarkable boutique boltholes and big brand hotels that excite and surprise, weaving rich narratives about their locations into unique schemes and solving design dilemmas in ingenious ways. I have found interpretations of industrial style in authentic conversions and new-builds. I have gathered many different style ideas for my home and for the homes of clients. Following the success of the first Warehouse Home book, which was released in 2017, it is high time we published a sequel. And with so many industrial-style hotels around the world, the topic for the next title has always been obvious. For me personally, it also feels like I have come full circle. I started my career in monthly magazines and would visit the best design shows, retail stores and workshops to source furniture, fabrics, accessories and lighting for photoshoots. I frequently found myself on location working with top photographers at envy-inducing homes. Later, I launched a luxury spa hotel guide for an international publisher, travelling extensively and visiting some of the world's most exciting hotels to enjoy indulgent spa treatments along the way. Almost a decade after my first magazine role, I spotted a gap in the market and took a leap to release a journal of my own. I had bought an apartment in a listed warehouse in East London and realised, while decorating it, that the industrial aesthetic was ubiquitous. It was clear to me that there was a need for a media brand and design studio that specialised in the urban loft look. Since Warehouse Home launched in 2014, we have often shared editorial features on hotels, from those housed in old factories to others in repurposed offices or custom-built. And our interior design studio has shared examples from the hospitality sector when discussing concepts for residential clients. Writing *Hotel To Home* has enabled me to combine my passions and my professional experiences. *Hotel To Home* is not a travel guide, it is a design manual for achieving hotel chic industrial style in any home. There are over 40 hotels featured in this book, in locations ranging from New York and Philadelphia, London and Sydney to Berlin, Cape Town and Singapore. There is a former sugar factory in China, a converted limestone works in Sweden and even a restored crane in Denmark. Hotel case studies have been compiled into five chapters: Structural Features, Materials, Colour, Feature Furnishings and Lighting.

> **"This is not a travel guide. It is a design manual filled with ideas for achieving hotel chic industrial style at home."**

Each case study is followed by a Real Home example or Get The Look section, in which a particular design element from the preceding hotel is explored in more detail, with our suggestions on how to apply each concept at home. The book draws modern and vintage ideas from these remarkable hotels and shares how to adapt them to any residential setting. There are plenty of solutions too for everyday interior design challenges, such as storage to suit compact spaces and how to use colour to transform a room. Whether you live in an industrial conversion or just aspire to that aesthetic, you will find ideas for every space and budget. A full list of homeware stockists is provided at the end. If you want to visit the locations featured to experience their distinctive interiors for yourself, the full details are provided on the hotels listing page to facilitate your travel plans. It has been a poignant experience compiling this book during the Coronavirus pandemic. The travel industry has suffered greatly. And successive lockdowns have meant that so many of us have been denied not only the opportunity to book holidays but even the chance to visit loved ones. As the world opens up to us all again, I hope this book helps you to experience every new destination, and your home, through a fresh creative lens.

Structural Features

From uncovered brickwork and textured concrete to exposed piping and factory windows, old industrial buildings offer many magnificent architectural features that set the scene for striking hotel interiors. Preserving and showcasing the fabric of these distinctive buildings enables architects and designers to weave a richer narrative into their schemes and create spaces that honour the past while impressing even the most well-travelled modern-day guests. In recent years, residential warehouse conversions have also become ever more covetable because those same authentic elements provide homeowners with an exciting creative challenge. And for those many others who aspire to achieving an industrial look at home, there are a number of clever ways to recreate the unique decorative impact of even the larger-scale structural features.

At The Eliza Jane, New Orleans, many large expanses of bare brickwork have been left untouched, while others have been treated to a coat of paint. The juxtaposition of raw and painted surfaces adds textural as well as visual interest, while the use of bold colours enhances the tone and character of the naked brick. The treatment reflects the building's individual history and the atmosphere of the city known as The Big Easy.

Yangshuo Sugar House

A REMARKABLE RETREAT IN CHINA CREATED FROM A FORMER SUGAR MILL

Renowned as a paradise on Earth, there is an almost other-worldly atmosphere around Yangshuo. Situated in the southeast of China, the area is characterised by its karst mountains, verdant hills and broad sweeping Yulong river. Amidst this dramatic scenery of lush mountainous terrain is an old sugar mill, built in the 1960s. The mill was originally rescued from demolition by the Alila hotel group, who had a singular vision for a unique resort. It took four years to convert the abandoned sugar mill. Beijing-based Vector architects, worked with Shenzen firm Horizontal Design, embracing the picturesque setting and the heritage features of the old mill. Existing structures were restored and repurposed for the public amenities. And new masonry extensions were added, housing the 177 guest rooms. The material palette of the new wings, including hollow concrete blocks and board-formed concrete, draws on the qualities of the surviving industrial architecture. The simple gabled profiles successfully avoid overshadowing the oddly romantic mill complex by gently echoing the heritage silhouette and completing a cluster of pitched roofs. Communist motivational slogans, stencilled onto the exterior walls of the 1960s buildings, have been carefully preserved. Inside, the fascinating story of Yangshuo and the mill is captured in photos and artworks from every era now on display throughout the lofty public spaces. Perspex flooring reveals softly illuminated old foundations. Many of the modern furnishings, such as rice paper and beech chairs, are also Chinese by design. A sense of aesthetic authenticity and yin and yang pervades throughout what is arguably one of the most spectacular hotels in China, where the new owners continue to embrace the property's industrial origins and its remarkable location.

1. The expansive ornamental ponds of the sunken plaza connect old and new architecture, reflected on the surface of the water. The resort looks even more beautiful against the mountainous backdrop in the faint light of dusk and dawn. At night, only the glow from the guest accommodation is visible.

2. The hotel's spectacular swimming pool is framed by a towering concrete truss, formerly used for loading sugar cane onto boats. The concrete columns create a material connection to the old industrial buildings in the background to the pool area, while contrasting with a natural stone setting.

3.

3. The original Sugar House is home to the hotel restaurant. Here, outdoor dining on the sizeable raised balcony offers the best of both worlds; the opportunity to soak up the atmospheric natural setting and to admire the characterful mill buildings.

4. The enormous floor-to-ceiling factory windows and an understated interior scheme, focused on natural timber, ensure that guests dining indoors can also savour the spectacular views. New glazing was matched to the former mill's original windows.

5. In the hotel's public spaces, the use of select bold colours challenges the mill buildings' features. The contrast between bare concrete and timber beams with a circular red seating area in the lobby is particularly striking. The sunken arrangement, with low-level lighting, successfully preserves the cavernous proportions of the old industrial space.

6.

6. Guest rooms, which are housed in the new wing, have private terraces with superb views. The use of timber and stone in the rooms references both the construction of the former mill and the hotel's natural surroundings. Bathroom walls were crafted from local rocks, while delicate friezes on bedroom walls depict the notable features of nearby Guilin.

GET THE LOOK

WAREHOUSE WINDOWS

Steel windows are often the distinguishing attributes of industrial conversions. Creating a strong urban look and flooding internal spaces with natural light, they are highly desirable architectural features and their influence is seen throughout the design world.

1 **USE INTERIOR GLAZING TO DIVIDE A LARGER AREA WITH A WOW-FACTOR WAREHOUSE-INSPIRED LOOK**
Belgian brand Portapivot specialises in the production of high-end architectural hardware for interior doors. Fixed glass partition walls, hinged doors and pivoting room dividers can be ordered in custom dimensions and with optional grid profiles. This soaring glass panel on a patented Portapivot hinge is an impressive way to separate two areas within a larger room while still retaining the effect of loft-inspired open-plan living.

3 **REFLECT NATURAL LIGHT BY USING A MIRROR**
This industrial curved top window mirror from Cox & Cox borrows its look from period fenestration. The panes of glass are individually framed by iron which has a lightly aged finish that enhances the mirror's vintage industrial appearance. The mirror was designed to be wall mounted in order to create the captivating illusion of an authentic warehouse window. It is an effective way to brighten even a narrow hallway but is equally well suited to living rooms and bedrooms.

2 **PICK FURNITURE DESIGNS, LARGE AND SMALL, THAT ARE INFLUENCED BY FACTORY WINDOWS**
This Frame cabinet by the Copenhagen-based interior design brand Louise Roe is handcrafted in Denmark. Produced in high quality heavy steel, the unit is sturdy and robust and its size and shape make it a versatile storage or display solution. The hinged glass door, divided into panels, mimics classic industrial glazing but the reference is subtle. The cabinet has a timeless design that will suit any room in any home.

4 **BRING FACTORY WINDOWS INTO BATHROOMS**
Styling the bathroom of this show apartment in Manchester, England, the Warehouse Home interior design team wanted to honour the heritage of the converted cotton mill and in particular draw attention to its original windows. Our studio commissioned Majestic Showers to create a nickel-coated version of their Metalwork Trellis shower screen. The panelled design immediately calls to mind warehouse windows, the nickel finish gives a refreshingly modern twist.

Hotel Cycle

A BOUTIQUE HOTEL IN A WAREHOUSE COMPLEX DEVOTED TO CYCLISTS

Known for its spectacular rolling hills and traditional wooden townhouses ('machiyas' in Japanese), the area surrounding the coastal city of Onomichi on Hiroshima island is popular with tourists, and particularly favoured by cyclists. The warehouses set along the Onomichi channel overlook the cargo ships entering and leaving the harbour and also enjoy views of the picturesque islands of Setouchi. One of the warehouses, Onomichi U2, now houses a complex dedicated to cycling. It comprises Hotel Cycle, a bar and restaurant, a café and a bakery, a specialist cycling clothing shop and a bike store. Japanese studio Suppose Design Office was responsible for the conversion of the waterfront warehouse. While the exterior appearance remains unaltered, the interior has been ingeniously transformed. As its name suggests, Hotel Cycle was conceived with the cyclist in mind.

Guests arriving on two wheels can cycle directly up to the 24-hour reception desk to check in and can even take their bicycles to their rooms. For those needing to carry out essential maintenance, there are rental tools and repair spaces available. Hotel Cycle offers simple yet stylish accommodation and the opportunity for guests to relax in a unique, interactive setting. The architects retained the warehouse's original shell and exposed the raw brickwork and concrete. The fit-out of the 2,000 square metre high-ceilinged warehouse interior was inspired by the marine building's identity and construction materials common to the area. Timber, mortar and steel utilised throughout the renovated warehouse recall the long tradition of shipbuilding and old houses of Onomichi. For cyclists seeking a place to rest weary limbs, Hotel Cycle has 28 minimalist guest rooms. But tourists and locals also find plenty to enjoy at industrial chic Onomichi U2.

1. A metal staircase leads to and from the principal concourse, with Hotel Cycle's 28 suites located over two levels. The industrial-style ceiling lights chosen to illuminate the public spaces reference the city of Onomichi's long history of shipbuilding.

2. Onomichi U2 is a superb example of adaptive reuse. The distinctive old marine warehouse now contains a complete interactive space. Its shops and Hotel Cycle can be directly accessed from the waterfront boardwalk as well as from the main road.

3. Stripped back to its raw concrete and brick shell, the seafront warehouse provided ample space for freestanding retail and dining units as well as Hotel Cycle. Original concrete columns and new wire-frame shelves partition sections of the old building.

4. Most of the guest rooms have cycle racks for guests to store their bikes, meaning the cycles serve as display pieces in the minimalist style suites. The bathrooms are open to the bedrooms, with wall-to-wall glazing and full-length curtains giving privacy.

INTERIOR GLAZING

Glass partition walls are an effective way to create modern interiors filled with natural light. Multi-paned internal glazing that mimics warehouse windows establishes a sense of open-plan living and immediately creates an impactful industrial-inspired dwelling.

GLAZED WALLS INJECT WOW-FACTOR INTO A SOHO LOFT

The tech entrepreneur owner of this apartment, in the Soho district of lower Manhattan, commissioned interior designer Becky Shea to renovate the 2,800 square foot home and realise its potential. The former printing factory's original elevator opens directly into the loft. Aged timber columns and beams immediately establish an authentic industrial aesthetic. Stucco was painstakingly chipped away to uncover further timber elements and some of the building's brickwork. The stairwell and elevator were stripped back to reveal their true steel forms. With the aim of complementing these older features, Becky Shea conceived glazed partition walls with blackened steel frames, reminiscent of classic factory windows and referencing the building's cast-iron façade. Radiators were sandblasted and repainted black to match the new glazing. Knocking through smaller rooms and inserting internal glazing draws more light into the home. The demarcation between the master bedroom and bathroom is truly dramatic. Recycled dimpled glass from a Detroit factory adds authenticity and gives privacy in the shower.

The Singular Patagonia

A CONVERTED REFRIGERATION FACTORY IN THE CHILEAN WILDERNESS

Created from the converted century-old cold storage plant Frigorifico Bories, The Singular Patagonia received a National Monument designation in 1996. The factory operated from 1915 to 1971. But following its inspired transformation, the site is today home to one of Chile's most remarkable hotels. Situated in a region of unparalleled natural beauty, overlooking the Last Hope Sound inlet and the Andes mountain peaks, The Singular Patagonia is a spectacular example of architectural adaptation, carved out of a sprawling old industrial building and benefiting from an impressive contemporary extension. The exterior and interior design reflects the natural surroundings, while also paying tribute to local history and customs and the legacy of the cold storage plant itself. Part of the original building now functions as a fascinating museum, with preserved machinery on display in the former engine room and visitors able to view the one-time tannery and blacksmith workshop. When the modern portion of the hotel was added to the existing factory, careful attention was paid to the design. The aim was to establish separate identities for the old and new buildings while also forming material links through the use of exposed concrete, bare wooden fixtures and the creation of open-plan spaces. The guest rooms offer understated, modern rustic luxury and unmatchable vistas. A comfortable and inviting reading room serves as an alternative setting from which to savour the scenery and the tranquillity of the hotel's remote setting. The spa, which has a heated pool, sauna, steam room and treatment rooms, completes the comprehensive offering for the modern-day traveller. But the real triumph of The Singular Patagonia is still the authentic integration of industrial heritage throughout the guests' experience.

1. Large windows offer guests spectacular views from every area of the hotel. Natural materials used throughout the interiors emphasise the sense of place and establish visual links to the outdoors.

2. The hotel is known for its fabulous food. The intimate *asador* (grill) is a raw industrial setting in which to watch the chefs at work and savour the finest Chilean barbequed beef, lamb and guanaco.

3. An enormous fireplace sets the scene in the open-plan lounge and restaurant. The soaring space is punctuated by towering timber columns, which lead to heavily beamed ceilings and offset bare brick walls. The cavernous space is filled with character and decorated in a fittingly rustic manner.

4. A museum has been incorporated into the hotel as a means of preserving key structures, equipment and artefacts in an authentic environment and for guests to learn about the plant's intriguing history.

5. The 54 spacious rooms and three larger suites all have pared-back interiors, with raw concrete ceilings and neutral décor, encouraging guests to savour the astonishing views of the Patagonian landscape through floor-to-ceiling picture windows.

TIMBER BEAMS

Exposed beams are a desirable feature, adding character to a property. Any evidence of age or wear and tear in the timber adds to the historic narrative of the building, while carefully considered modern additions will ensure the beams are highlighted successfully.

A DRAMATIC SHOWCASE OF HISTORIC BEAMS AND MACHINES

Architecture studio Anna and Eugeni Bach converted a nineteenth-century chocolate factory in La Bisbal, Spain, into this family home and studio. With minimal interventions, the architects were able to convert the brick and stone property's interior into cool and inviting living spaces. The three floors of the former factory are connected by an original staircase at one end of the building and a new set of stairs at the other. Each of the levels displayed a different construction technique, the most dramatic of which were the brick-vaulted and timber-beamed ceilings. These elements were painstakingly preserved and now provide character and visual impact in every area of the home. Crisp white walls and minimal décor maximise natural light while highlighting the historic language of the former factory.

The Eliza Jane

A BOUTIQUE HOTEL BREATHING NEW LIFE INTO OLD WAREHOUSES IN THE BIG EASY

The Eliza Jane is built within seven historic warehouses in the Central Business District of New Orleans, just two and a half blocks from the famed French Quarter. The brief to the New York-based architecture and interior design studio Stonehill Taylor had been to create a quintessentially New Orleans hotel, but the precise interpretation was left open. Stonehill Taylor began by researching the previous occupants of the old warehouse buildings. They included Antoine Peychaud, the original and renowned mixologist, who packaged his infamous bitters on the site. Gulf Baking Soda company and Peters Cartridge shop are also known to have used the old warehouses. And yet, while the original intention had been to celebrate each of these former occupants in the hotel's design, Stonehill Taylor were drawn to one particularly fascinating tenant. In 1876, Eliza Jane

Nicholson assumed ownership of New Orleans' *Daily Picayune* paper. Over the coming years, she transformed a penny paper from near bankruptcy into an American institution. So, it was the legacy of the nation's trailblazing first female newspaper publisher that Stonehill Taylor chose to honour at 315 Magazine Street. And the publishing references begin on arrival, with index card cabinets repurposed as a reception desk and given a transformative coat of paint. Vintage typewriters and bespoke wall murals weave an ongoing narrative for guests to discover. The public lounges channel Spanish courtyard architecture while celebrating interconnected warehouse structures. Exposed brickwork throughout the hotel is offset by coloured plaster, russet tones, mismatched velvets, marble accents, crocodile leather and abundant greenery. The result is a boutique-style hotel with an inviting romantic-industrial ambience that is uniquely New Orleans.

1. In the lobby, steel columns and bare brick walls are complemented by an elegant colour palette that centres on shades of blue and purple. Exposed timbers contrast with parquet flooring to establish a sense of refined industrial style in the old factory.

2. While much of the exposed brickwork has been left bare, many of the other walls and architectural features have been painted in vibrant tones that actually draw attention to the heritage brick. New parquet and tiled floors also suit the old buildings.

3. The hotel's main public space features a 60-foot high atrium, flooded with natural light. Slate blue plaster walls and jewel-toned velvet sofas combine with Persian rugs in a space that exudes industrial chic and captures the unique spirit of New Orleans.

4. The Eliza Jane offers many useful lessons in the effectiveness of juxtaposing bare and painted brick walls. Combining these treatments enhances the rich textural quality of spaces. Structural metal wall ties, with oversized rivets, are also noteworthy.

5. Carpet with a pattern and tone that evokes old concrete or distressed plaster is ideal for areas with exposed brick. The deep colours on feature walls and in upholstery, as well as touches of brass, bring a sophisticated elegance into the hotel's 196 rooms.

6. Three walls in this guest room have each been given a different treatment. The lovely wallpaper was custom-designed by the Stonehill Taylor team and shows a large repeating pattern of Acanthus leaves. This feature area is 'framed' with a picture rail.

7. In the sophisticated monochromatic bathrooms, high-gloss bevelled-edge metro tiles with matching white grout maximise light and call to mind the expanses of exposed brickwork seen throughout the hotel. The juxtaposition of these smooth wall tiles with the matt hexagonal floor tiles is modern yet timeless. The smaller hexagons indicate entry into a self-contained wet area or an open shower.

8. Double doors with frosted glass panels open into this Editor's Suite oversized bathroom, creating an added sense of drama. Wall-to-wall glass, with an incorporated hinged door, effectively separates the bathroom into two distinctive spaces and cleverly creates an enclosed wet room that features dual shower fixtures and a luxurious soaking bathtub.

"Highlighting the building's heritage features created a unique experience for hotel guests."

BETHANY GALE, STONEHILL TAYLOR

GET THE LOOK

PAINTED BRICKWORK

Exposed brick is immediately effective when pursuing an industrial scheme in any home, as the fabric of the building is laid bare. Painting brickwork draws further attention to raw walls, emphasising their textural quality, and highlights other architectural features.

1 **APPLY BOLDER COLOURS FOR A GREATER IMPACT**
When designing this show apartment in London, the Warehouse Home interior design studio aimed to reveal a different side to warehouse living. A principal aim was to challenge the notion that exposed brickwork, which has become synonymous with industrial interiors and all the rage in interior design, can be treated in only one or two simple ways. The brickwork in this former factory, for example, had been given a conventional treatment and was either bare or painted white. Warehouse Home dramatically transformed the rooms with colour. Dark blue paint was applied to the lower walls of the living area. The upper walls were painted a rich, but lighter, blue. This decorative decision helped to enhance the scale and drama of the space, surprising and exciting visitors.

2 **OFFSET RAW CONCRETE WITH A DEEPER COLOUR**
While there was no exposed concrete in the old factory building, the Warehouse Home interior design studio team opted to give more character to an unassuming side wall, applying a hyper-realistic concrete-effect wallpaper. With the mural in place, this small wall section suddenly made a visual impact. Blue-painted brickwork and faux concrete contrasted strikingly. A piping clothes rail was fitted as the finishing touch for an area that now had style as well as a clear purpose.

3 **DRAW ATTENTION TO STRUCTURAL FEATURES**
Simple white paintwork can balance rough bricks. But deep paint colours on brick alongside raw walls can serve to highlight interesting architectural features. In this show apartment, Warehouse Home interior design studio drew attention to the enormous factory windows by painting the recesses blue. Though used sparingly, the flashes of colour connected this dining space to the rest of the open-plan apartment, while unpainted walls demarked a distinctive space.

1.

2.

The Audio

INDUSTRIAL INFLUENCE AND EARTHY TONES IN COPENHAGEN'S CREATIVE HYBRID

Danish design brand Menu collaborated with renowned studio Norm Architects to establish hybrid hotel and concept store The Audo in Copenhagen. The Audo is situated in a century-old building, comprising a former boathouse and Neo-Baroque residence, in the city's Nordhavn district. The north harbour has a rich industrial history but has also become the city's hotspot for modern architecture and gastronomic highlights. Norm Architects determined to preserve the building's original façade in order to honour its heritage. Inside, by contrast, there was an industrial concrete structure. At ground level, nearly all of the partition walls were knocked through to form a large open-plan warehouse-style space. Oversized concrete floor tiles were laid and perforated black metal panels used to clad the ceilings. Tactile seating in a neutral palette softens the industrial chic

scheme. Audo is an acronym of the Latin phrase *ab uno disce omnes* ("from one, learn all"), and the hotel's name is a nod to its multi-functional spaces. In addition to a ground-floor living room-style area, there is also a small café, a restaurant and the hotel's concept store, where everything at The Audo is available for purchase, from cushions to robes, furniture to literature, and the works of emerging and established creatives are showcased alongside products from Menu and other selected brands. A staircase leads from the ground floor to the Menu offices and communal workspace, while hotel guests take a lift to the ten rooms in the building's former attic. And whereas the pervading aesthetic on the ground floor is industrial and raw, as visitors ascend through the building the atmosphere becomes more intimate, the choice of materials warmer in texture and tone. From top to bottom, The Audo is an inspirational design destination.

3.

1. Part gallery, part store, the Audo Concept is a continually evolving design environment. From the furniture and lighting in the communal spaces to the linens and accessories on display in the suites, The Audo's décor can be purchased here for home.

2. The grey marble bar-cum-concierge area and concrete floor tiles enhance the industrial aesthetic established by the sizeable factory-style windows. White bouclé sofas and velvet armchairs introduce more tactile elements within the minimalist spaces.

3. The boutique hotel's attic guest rooms are each uniquely configured and are decorated with Menu furniture, lighting and accessories. The original timber beams add charm and character, framing and highlighting key areas of the accommodation.

4. Danish paint and plaster firm St. Leo conceived ten bespoke Dolomite Plaster colours for The Audo, inspired by the area's rich heritage. A chalky finish suits the tranquil rooms, with soft earthy tones complemented by pale Dinesen oak flooring.

GET THE LOOK

GET THE LOOK

RAW PLASTER

Raw plaster is perfect for warehouse conversions and loft-style spaces. Its textural quality works beautifully with exposed concrete or bare brickwork and larger expanses set the tone for a pared-back aesthetic. Delicate shades are ideal for creating softer industrial schemes.

1 EMBRACE THE MUTED PINK OF SETTING PLASTER

Husband-and-wife team Zoe Chan Eayrs and Merlin Eayrs do not work on client projects. Instead, the two architects initiate their own spaces, which they live in and then sell before moving on to a new scheme. With no client brief to fulfil, they have total creative freedom, but a consistent theme is a sense of retreat from the outside. In New Cross Lofts, in London, pink shades were selected for their calming effect and earthy plaster is also a nod to Morocco, where the couple married.

2 CHOOSE A DISTINCTIVE SHADE AND GIVE BOTH WALLS AND CEILINGS A REFRESHING MAKEOVER

When architects Chan and Eayrs commenced work on The Beldi, a three-bedroom lateral apartment in a converted shoe factory in Shoreditch, East London, they wanted to create a calm oasis from the urban jungle below. Raw lime plaster harmonises with other materials chosen for their tactile characteristics, including cross-sawn limed timber and textured tiles and bricks. Soft green ceilings, columns and walls reference the verdant treetop views, drawing the natural world inside.

3 HANG PLASTER PANELS AS ORIGINAL ARTWORK

Decorative plaster artist Tanya Vacarda uses a trowel like a paintbrush to create original plaster-on-canvas murals, wall coverings and artworks. It is a distinctive new treatment for the traditional building material and the craft of Italian plasterers and fresco artists. By blending pigments with Italian plaster and applying it in thin layers, Vacarda makes beautiful pieces with organic surface textures and colour patterns. The creations are uniquely pliable as well as reusable.

Ovolo Southside

A FORMER WAREHOUSE TRANSFORMED INTO A VIBRANT CREATIVE HUB

Set in the Wong Chuk Hang district, Ovolo Southside is Hong Kong's first warehouse conversion hotel. Locally based British architect Paul Kember, director of KplusK Associates, was commissioned to bring to life the vision of hotelier Girish Jhunjhnuwala. The concept drew on the creative spirit of the surrounding area as well as the industrial transformation of Hong Kong, while also imaginatively channelling the character of the former warehouse. Guests are introduced to the building's past from the moment they arrive. It retains its concrete exterior, as well as vast expanses of raw concrete inside. The large reception desks are constructed from machinery parts. Steel pipes and foil-clad ducting, left uncovered, fortify the authentic industrial look. Yet against the raw grey surfaces and bare metal, there are also bold splashes of dazzling colour. The edgy neighbourhood setting

prompted KPlusK Associates and Ovolo to enlist several Chinese and international artists to contribute to the transformation of the old warehouse. Ovolo Southside is, as a result, an engaging blend of hip hotel and design destination. Corridors are adorned with playful graphic motifs and urban graffiti-inspired designs. Art installations are showcased in the public spaces. Colour is used sparingly, but with impact, in the loft-like guest accommodation. Plaster ceilings and exposed services establish a strong utilitarian look, which is complemented by furniture designs inspired by steel workbenches and tool boxes. The building's old windows were replaced with full-height glazing, which maximises natural light and capitalises fully on the views. Ovolo Southside is an art-lover's dream, and it has been integral to the rise of Wong Chuk Hang as a cultural district. But its industrial chic interiors capture the best of modern Hong Kong too.

1. Wong Chuk Hang is also known as the South Island Cultural District, in part due to its large number of art galleries. Vibrant and edgy art installations appear throughout Ovolo Southside, including a portrait of The Beatles' John Lennon, painstakingly crafted using thumb tacks.

2. The former warehouse still retains its concrete exterior. Inside, vast expanses of exposed concrete also remain, but the raw grey surfaces are offset by splashes of colour. Adjustable Lampe Gras floor lamps by DCW éditions provide focused lighting and suit the lounge's urban vibe.

"We took a detail-orientated approach to the architecture and thought outside the box."

PAUL KEMBER, KPLUSK ASSOCIATES

3. Steel-framed furniture and a heavy-duty communal table form a centrepiece in the Komune lounge. Jazzy artworks depicting Hong Kong's high-rises and colourful seat upholstery create a lively atmosphere within a raw industrial space.

4. Architect Paul Kember preserved the building's original internal structure, meaning each of the 162 guest rooms has a unique format. The New York loft look is consistent throughout, completed by heavy-duty black fixtures and fittings.

5. Slatted screens serve as room dividers while retaining the sense of open-plan living and enabling the flow of natural light throughout the space. The patterns are reminiscent of breeze blocks and suit the plaster ceilings and bare brick walls.

REAL HOME

POLISHED CONCRETE

A smooth concrete floor immediately creates a strong industrial aesthetic, but it also has several practical benefits. Once the raw concrete has been polished and sealed, it becomes a sleek non-porous surface that is durable, easy to clean and ideal for allergy sufferers.

EMBRACE POLISHED CONCRETE FLOORS THROUGHOUT OPEN-PLAN LIVING SPACES FOR AN AUTHENTIC EFFECT

Javelin Block is a design and building company based in Birmingham, in the English Midlands. Since 2010, the firm has been responsible for the reanimation of much of the city's Jewellery Quarter, a district home to Europe's largest number of surviving nineteenth and twentieth-century jewellery buildings. Derwent Works is one such project; a Victorian metal works rescued from dereliction and sensitively converted by Javelin Block into four apartments. Each loft has a unique layout and original features were retained or restored throughout. Brick walls and steel beams were left exposed. New steel-framed windows replaced the existing fenestration and returned the building to its former glory. In the open-plan living, kitchen and dining area of each loft, the concrete flooring instantly creates a strong industrial tone that suits the old building. But modern under-floor heating has also been installed. Metal-clad kitchens mimic the finish of polished concrete. Salvaged factory lights complete the impressive heritage conversion.

1.

The Waterhouse At South Bund

A DISUSED JAPANESE ARMY HEADQUARTERS NOW CAPTURES THE SPIRIT OF SHANGHAI

Set in Shanghai's South Bund district, and fronting the Huangpu River, The Waterhouse is a boutique hotel in a converted 1930s building. Once the Japanese army's headquarters, it was renovated by celebrated Shanghai-based practice Neri&Hu Design and Research Office. The architectural concept at the heart of the redevelopment was that a differentiation should be made between what already existed and what was new. The original three-storey concrete building was restored. Additions were made using Corten steel, forming a clear visual distinction and striking contrast with the raw concrete, as well as reflecting the industrial past of the riverside docks. Neri&Hu also designed a steel-clad fourth floor on the roof, inspired by the giant cargo ships passing along the river. The hotel's interior was similarly influenced by history and local culture. Of the 19 individual guest rooms, nine offer Bund waterfront views. The remaining ten rooms face inwards, offering aspects into the hotel lobby, restaurant or bar. Narrow apertures, enabling glimpses between the private and public spaces, mimic the experience of walking along Shanghai's narrow 'longtang' laneways bordered by tightly packed housing. And just as Shanghai itself offers an intoxicating combination of old and new, Neri&Hu cleverly blended historic architecture, antique furniture and modern designs throughout The Waterhouse. The minimalist interiors, characterised by the textures and tones of raw concrete, showcase furniture by Finn Juhl, Arne Jacobsen and Hans Wegner. The Waterhouse At South Bund is conveniently located for the Cool Docks development, filled with culinary hotspots and trendy bars. But the interiors of The Waterhouse, which capture the very essence of this bustling metropolis, make it one of Shanghai's hottest hotels.

1. The old windows were replaced and new elongated glass panels were inserted at points around the hotel, offering glimpses into guest rooms from the lobby and dining hall. This approach encourages guests to see beyond the building, bringing to mind the interconnected lanes that define Shanghai's unique character.

2. The lobby feels like a courtyard. Its raw concrete walls and structural steels set a strong industrial tone. The sparing use of décor ensures these original features remain the focus. A Paper Chandelier by Studio Job for Moooi, crafted from paper, papier-mâché and cardboard, is a statement against the bare utilitarian backdrop.

3. Throughout the hotel there is a blurring and an inversion of interior and exterior spaces. Visual links are also established between the different areas within the guest rooms, which are defined by their clean lines. In this suite, the bath and shower have been enclosed within a glass cube, which also doubles as a room divider.

> "The architectural concept rested on achieving a clear contrast between old and new."

NERI&HU

GET THE LOOK

RAW CONCRETE

Hyper-realistic wallpapers and murals are an effective way to achieve an industrial look, without the expense and effort of exposing raw concrete. There are a multitude of designs on the market, in a variety of colours, and there are creative ways to apply them.

1 WALLPAPER THE CEILING FOR A DISTINCTIVE LOOK

The ceiling is often referred to as the 'fifth wall'. Taking a creative approach to the ceiling, and applying a concrete-effect mural, is an ingenious way to transform a room with a touch of pattern. It offers the opportunity to keep the walls plain and a space minimalist, while still adding character and visual interest. This Battered Wall paper by Rebel Walls is based on a surface in a café, discovered by the brand's team. On the ceiling, it draws the eye up and makes this room look more spacious.

2 USE MURAL DESIGNS WITH LIFELIKE DETAILING

In this factory conversion apartment, Warehouse Home chose the Cracked Concrete mural by Surface View to complement the reclaimed timber floorboards and enhance the industrial aesthetic. The paper was positioned in order that a substantial vertical 'crack' would highlight an original wall-mounted radiator. Wooden furniture with interesting forms and an antique armchair upholstered in vibrant mustard yellow velvet contrast strikingly with the concrete-style wall.

3 FIND CONCRETE DESIGNS INCLUDING COLOUR

The digitally printed wallpaper murals by Swedish brand Mr Perswall have no limitations when it comes to shape, repeats or colour. Painted Concrete Wall gives the convincing impression of an aged concrete wall, originally painted green, where the paint has cracked and flaked away over time. Captured Reality depicts a concrete wall painted in two different tones. The horizontal division makes a striking backdrop in any room and can be utilised to frame key furniture.

4 CHOOSE WEATHERWORN EXTERIOR DESIGNS

Multi-award-winning wallpaper studio Robin Sprong works with designers, illustrators and photographers for a diverse collection of wall murals. The Cape Town-based firm offers a full range of concrete-inspired prints, all of which can be altered to precise measurements required. Grout and Off The Slab both appear remarkably true to life, depicting rugged joins, rust marks and stains caused by weather. A selection of finishes enhances the realistic appearance.

1.

The Hoxton Williamsburg

A STYLISH AND SOCIABLE DESTINATION WITH A STRONG SENSE OF PLACE

The Hoxton Williamsburg is a nine-storey hotel located on the site of the old Rosenwach factory. Rosenwach is the oldest water tower company in America, producing iconic wooden rooftop water tanks for over 150 years. Once an industrial area, Williamsburg has experienced dramatic gentrification over the last decade, its former warehouses now occupied by trendy restaurants, clothing stores and apartments. While The Hoxton Williamsburg was the boutique hotel brand's first foray into America, the signature Hoxton aesthetic translated comfortably from the London original to the new Brooklyn outpost. There is a considered blending of urban style with aspects of a hip members club. Hotel owner Ennismore has paid careful attention to the site's history and to the diversity and distinctive character of the surrounding area. The most obvious nod to the old Rosenwach building is on the ground floor, where the restaurant was formed around a realistic reconstruction of the former water tower factory's carriage house. The sunken ground-floor lobby, which is open to the central bar and restaurant, is predominantly public space. Two large fireplaces set the scene for cosy winter evenings, while vintage sofas and luxurious velvet armchairs invite guests to linger and relax. A delicate palette of neutrals and pastel shades, set against the light parquet flooring, successfully completes the soft industrial scheme. Subtle references to an industrial past and urban setting appear in the guest rooms too. Subway bathroom tiles are distinctly industrial, while Art Deco forms and velvet upholstered headboards edge the aesthetic towards sophisticated boutique hotel. Williamsburg has been fashionable for over twenty years. The Hoxton has certainly enhanced the area's appeal for those journeying from near and far.

1-3. Ennismore collaborated with Soho-House on schemes for public areas, including the sunken ground-floor lobby which is open to everyone. The hotel's main restaurant is formed around a convincing recreation of the factory's old carriage house. The use of exposed brickwork, huge steel columns and timber establishes the industrial connection.

4. Clever storage solutions abound in the guest rooms. Wall-mounted brass rails are an industrial luxe touch and provide plenty of hanging space. The large beds have drawers.

5. Floor-to-ceiling windows flood the 175 guest rooms with natural light while offering captivating views of Brooklyn or the iconic Manhattan skyline. The bespoke bed linen by local Brooklyn brand Dusen Dusen has black and white line motifs such as ladders and steps, forming the letters in Hoxton. The graphic design befits the hotel's urban vibe.

GET THE LOOK

BOLT DETAILS

Structural steels immediately establish a strong industrial aesthetic in a hotel or residential conversion. But for those seeking to create the look without this heavy-duty architectural feature, there are impactful furniture and lighting designs that will measure up to the task.

1 CHOOSE UNASHAMEDLY INDUSTRIAL CREATIONS

Steel Vintage is a family-run furniture business based in Bristol, England. The city is famous for its links to the nineteenth-century engineer Isambard Kingdom Brunel, whose work is visible across Bristol and includes the instantly recognisable Clifton Suspension Bridge. Brunel's remarkable feats of engineering have clearly influenced Steel Vintage in their furniture design. From kitchen cabinets and coffee tables to desks, beds and benches, every Steel Vintage design displays a strong industrial form. Each item of furniture is handmade to order and can be modified to match the customer's precise requirements. The Brunel range, inspired by the master of engineering, pays homage to the Victorian icon with pieces that bear his name (below right). The substantial Brunel desk offsets polished steel with a vintage wood desktop. Raised on brass-plated adjustable feet, it also features raw as well as brass-plated bolts. The Kingsbridge table (below left) fuses aspects of industrial bridge designs with steampunk exuberance for a big-impact dining setting to impress any guest.

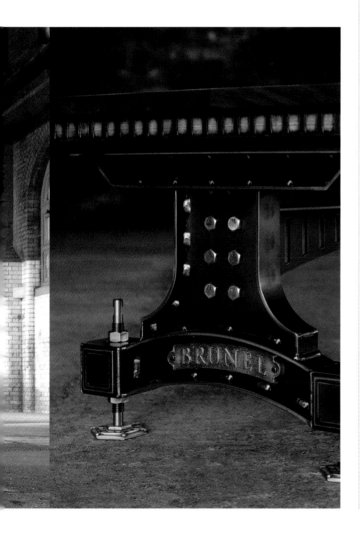

2 USE LIGHTING DESIGNS WITH BOLT ELEMENTS

(Top row) The Retro Industrial C1720 pendant by Italian brand Ferroluce is an angular design constructed in metal and available in various colours. Screws form an essential aspect of the design. The Rivet round pendant by Darklight Design is hand cast in concrete and offers a raw industrial lighting solution. (Middle row) Aged brass and acrylic contrast strikingly in the Hunts Point lamp by Hudson Valley Lighting. The Bolt table lamp by Tonone, from Darklight Design, acts as a smart bedside lamp. (Bottom row) The Mumford wall light by Pooky can be fitted pointing up or down and suits a traditional shade. The Button Light by Flos looks effective fixed in groups on walls or ceilings.

Gorgeous George

A CELEBRATION OF ARCHITECTURAL HERITAGE AND SHOWCASE FOR LOCAL CULTURE

Located in Cape Town's vibrant inner city, Gorgeous George is a 32-room design-led boutique hotel. Local architects Urbane Citizen oversaw the conversion of two iconic buildings, one Art Deco and one Edwardian, successfully repurposing the historic structures while generating a strong industrial narrative. Grand architraves, cornices and oak flooring reflect the aesthetic of two historic buildings. But they are juxtaposed with steel beams and sculptural concrete. The Johannesburg-based interior designer Tristan du Plessis embraced these rich architectural features and raw urban elements with a darker neutral palette punctuated by the occasional use of deep blue. And the concept for the public spaces and guest rooms was not derivative. Rather than importing the artwork and interior design elements, du Plessis opted to represent South African creatives throughout the hotel. Curated objects and furniture include those by David Krynauw, Gregor Jenkin and Egg Designs. The approach to the interiors reflects the hotel's ethos. Gorgeous George has been designed to attract international travellers as well as locals, offering visitors an authentic experience of lively Cape Town while mingling with the city's residents. This kind of hotel culture is a relatively new concept for South Africa, but it is clearly already proving popular. The open-plan bar, restaurant and lounge, which was conceived as 'a living room for the neighbourhood', offers guests a welcoming environment for socialising, with a dynamic and buzzy atmosphere. The contemporary yet timeless spaces lead to a rooftop pool on a raised deck, with further seating and a part-covered area that serves as a quiet hideaway. In what was once an under-explored part of Cape Town, Gorgeous George is a hip hotel with a distinct identity.

1. Vintage Jieldé lighting appears in the hotel's public spaces and rooms. The robust articulating lamps, first designed in 1953 for factories in France, are particularly desirable today for their bold look.

2. The interlinking spaces on the hotel's sixth floor combine raw concrete walls and exposed pipes with tactile wood panelling, touches of warm brass and leather upholstery for an urban chic aesthetic.

3. & 4. High-gloss white metro tiles are a classic solution for a vintage industrial-style bathroom. Monochrome penny tiles are a Victorian influence. Some of the guest suites have a bathtub in the room.

5. Furniture designer Gregor Jenkin created one of the most eye-catching features in the hotel's guest bathrooms; the handmade stainless steel legs which serve to support the custom-designed basins.

6. The high-ceilinged guest rooms, with painted overhead pipework, feature furniture and artworks by local creatives. South African artist David Brits is well-known for his sculptural works throughout his native city of Cape Town. Brits' hand-painted artwork, applied directly to the guest room walls, is based upon twisting and turning snakes, but is also reminiscent of urban graffiti. The thick black lines add drama to cool industrial-style accommodation.

> "By stripping back the layers, we uncovered the beautiful patina of the old buildings."
>
> TRISTAN DU PLESSIS

GET THE LOOK

PAINTED PIPEWORK

Exposed pipework is often considered out of place or inconvenient by interior designers and homeowners. But painting pipes can solve logistical issues and help to highlight other features. For those who like the idea, there are ways to get the look on a smaller scale too.

1 SOURCE COLOURFUL PIPING HOMEWARE DESIGNS

The Pipework Series by British designer Nick Fraser is a quirky collection of candle holders and coat racks. The concept began as an installation piece for coats and hats, a functional sculpture that appeared to be plumbed into the water system. Made in industrial materials typically used in plumbing work, the original idea has evolved into a series of practical and appealing designs available in various colours and finishes. The range is a celebration of exposed pipework to suit any home.

3 SELECT CONTRASTING OR MATCHING COLOURS

Brazilian studio SuperLimão renovated this apartment inside the modernist Saint Honoré Building, located in downtown São Paulo. Exposed pipes painted pale blue contrast strikingly with salmon pink ceilings and with the darker blue-pigmented concrete kitchen countertop. In the bedroom, the pastel exposed pipework complements the ocean-inspired wallpaper design. If drawing inspiration from this approach, consider also painting radiators and mouldings to match.

2 WITHIN A MONOCHROME INTERIOR SCHEME, HIGHLIGHT PIPEWORK IN AN ACCENT COLOUR

When Hong Kong studio Lim + Lu converted a former print factory into a loft apartment for an artist couple, they chose a vibrant shade of red to add visual interest by highlighting just the overhead pipes. This approach cleverly emphasises the soaring ceiling heights by drawing the eye upwards. The flash of red, viewed through their glass panes, also calls attention to a set of enormous industrial sliding doors.

Materials

Choosing the most appropriate materials for an interior design project requires careful consideration of the heritage and existing characteristics of the building. Thought should also be given to the desired aesthetic and mood. Mixed metals, wire mesh and polished concrete can be natural choices for former industrial buildings. But the creative challenge presented by these properties is frequently to soften original features to create welcoming accommodation. The secret to a successful scheme is often to offset raw or 'cold' surfaces like plaster, concrete and steel, with 'warmer' tactile materials. Reclaimed timber and stone-washed linen suit older spaces, but they also put a modern rustic twist on industrial style. Supple leather and sumptuous velvets immediately elevate an interior to 'industrial luxe'. These principles are equally valid and easily applied in any environment, whether in an authentic industrial conversion or for any room concept where a strong loft look is desired.

The Warehouse Hotel offers visitors and locals alike a uniquely Singaporean experience. Local firm Asylum drew inspiration from the building's history when designing spaces that would look and feel authentic. Furniture upholstered in brown leather suits the colours and textures of the open-plan lobby, where many original industrial features, including steel trusses and brick walls, were carefully preserved.

1.

2.

Veriu Broadway

SERVICED APARTMENTS IN SYDNEY FULL OF WAREHOUSE CHARACTER

Located in Sydney's Ultimo suburb, Veriu Broadway has the bustle of Broadway right on its doorstep with some of the city's best shops and restaurants. There are 64 serviced apartments in the old federation warehouse, which was formerly used as a tannery. It was converted into the apartment hotel in 2017. Local architecture firm JSA Studio (formerly Jones Sonter) retained the existing timber floor framing and a lightweight extension of upper floors was added under a sculptural zinc-clad roof. Inside, the principal objective was to achieve a balance between the character of the warehouse and spaces that were warm and inviting. Exposed industrial elements throughout Veriu Broadway reference the building's past. Aged structural timbers, steels, brickwork, concrete and piping have all been left uncovered. But against this backdrop, the award-winning architecture and interior design practice Mostaghim introduced sleek plywood joinery and leather upholstery. While colour is used sparingly, vintage furniture brings both comfort and a richness to the accommodation. Each of the self-contained apartments offers cool loft-inspired living and the atmosphere of a home away from home. Guest rooms on the hotel's first three floors have high ceilings with exposed beams and polished concrete floors. Other rooms also offer plenty of character, as well as views of the Central Business District. Every suite has a fully equipped kitchen and plenty of space for work or relaxation. Veriu hosts greet guests upon arrival and are on hand to help them experience the best the city has to offer. Living local is at the heart of the Veriu brand DNA. Veriu Broadway is equally well suited to younger travellers and the young at heart, who will savour the hotel's urban aesthetic and convenient location in equal measure.

1. & 2. Veriu's on-site café, The Hide, is set in the lobby and was designed as an informal meeting place for the neighbourhood. The large artwork on one side was stencilled directly onto the wall by famed Melbourne-based artist Logan Moody. It almost suggests a viewing hole into another world.

3. A plywood unit is a clever solution for this living room, effectively drawing attention from the wall-mounted television. An incorporated shelf offers convenient storage space. The design is ideal for an industrial-style interior and striking framed by raw brickwork, distressed timber and structural concrete.

4. A sleek contemporary kitchen makes a bold statement against aged timber and bare brickwork. The strong black units are matched by the classic bentwood chairs used in the open-plan dining area.

5. An L-shaped plywood structure serves as a room divider, with a leather-upholstered bench between the living area and the bedroom. The arrangement ensures the original beams remain the key feature.

6. In this bedroom, the smooth surfaces and clean lines of the bespoke joinery and headboard panel contrast successfully with the time-worn elements and a bedside table crafted from reclaimed wood.

PLYWOOD

The light tones, texture and sustainability of plywood make it a firm favourite with designers. While plywood furniture has been in production for over 170 years, modern-day architects are finding ways to showcase the material on a more dramatic scale.

USE PLYWOOD FOR SELECTED FEATURES IN A MODERN HOME AND AS A MATERIAL LINK TO AN INDUSTRIAL PAST

This distinctive modern home is set within a Grade II listed former wine warehouse in the heart of the old mill town Bradford on Avon, south-west England. Klas Hyllén Architecture designed the four-bedroom residence around a staircase which is suspended through a triple-height void and clad in birch plywood. The staircase is a bold architectural insertion. Its design is unapologetically contemporary and yet the material choice also displays a sensitivity to the heritage of the building and its original features. Exposed brickwork serves as an immediate visual reminder of the building's history. While some brick surfaces, such as a feature wall in the kitchen, have been left bare, most are painted white. The treatment maximises natural light while retaining the authentic industrial character of the brickwork. Against this bright backdrop, the plywood staircase and kitchen units create a chic industrial look with discernible Scandinavian influence. The factory-style glazing on the upper floors offer views of the dramatic new plywood staircase.

2.

Ace Hotel Downtown Los Angeles

A HIPSTER HOTEL THAT JUXTAPOSES A VARIETY OF DESIGN INFLUENCES AND AN INDUSTRIAL BACKDROP

T he 182-room Ace Hotel Downtown Los Angeles is housed within the United Artists Building. Built in 1927 as offices for the renowned film studio, the 13-storey Gothic icon was partly inspired by the Sagrada Família in Barcelona. The restoration of the historic building was led by Los Angeles architecture and interiors studio Commune Design, which has successfully combined old elements with locally inspired and modern interventions. The famous building is located at the heart of Downtown Los Angeles, in the rapidly gentrifying but still slightly edgy Broadway Theatre District. Commune Design's concept juxtaposed design elements inspired by hedonistic 1920s Hollywood, the resurgence of modernism in Los Angeles and the city's punk period in the 1980s. The building had been stripped of all interiors, leaving an almost brutalist structure. Commune Design

embraced these expanses of raw concrete, giving the hotel's public spaces and guest rooms a decidedly industrial edge that suits diverse and quirky design additions. To further localise the interiors, most of the custom furnishings and lighting were sourced, designed or made in California and neighbouring Mexico. And several local artists and artisans were recruited, their contributions ranging from charcoal portraits on plaster walls to felt sculptures and bespoke ceramics. The result is a destination with a rich narrative and layered interiors that reflect on the distinctive architectural and cultural history of Los Angeles. And there is the unmistakable influence of the Ace Hotel collective too. Music is at the heart of the brand and many of the guest rooms offer Martin Guitars, Ace x Rega turntables and a collection of vinyl records. It seems the building constructed for a maverick film studio will be a Los Angeles landmark for years to come.

"We treat every client as a creative collaborator and focus on what's best for the architecture or the space."

ROMAN ALONSO, COMMUNE DESIGN

1. The hotel's restaurant, Best Girl, was named after the first film screened at the United Artists Theatre in 1927. It has rapidly become a popular LA haunt and is revered as much for its design as for its globally influenced menu of eclectic dishes.

2. Dark green tongue-and-groove panelling in the mezzanine lounge creates an intimate environment within which to savour an evening drink. Black wooden seating with mid-century modern shapes offsets the exposed pipework painted in deep black.

3. Bespoke designed Pendleton wool blankets, with colourful blocks of colour, adorn the beds and are complemented by the yellow carpets. The rooms have otherwise been decorated in neutral tones, ensuring the concrete ceilings remain the highlight.

4. Homasote panels fixed to the walls serve two practical purposes, providing soundproofing and warmth. The soft tone and tactile nature of the material also suit the raw industrial elements and pared-back aesthetic of the guest accommodation.

4.

HOMASOTE

Homasote is a sustainable lightweight building board formed from recycled paper.
It provides soundproofing and insulation, but it is also a versatile and durable decorating
material that can be used for creative surfaces and notice boards of all shapes and sizes.

1 GET CREATIVE WITH WALL-TO-WALL HOMASOTE

Stephanie Housley, founder of well-loved brand Coral & Tusk, designs beautifully embroidered textiles for the home. Each piece begins as a pencil drawing, which is then machine-embroidered onto natural linen. In 2016, after nearly two decades living and working in New York, Stephanie and her husband relocated to Wyoming. Their mountain home features a separate studio, formerly a woodshed, which Stephanie has transformed into an enviable work space. Wall-to-wall homasote panels enable the designer to tack a huge array of cuttings and inspirational images alongside works-in-progress and completed designs. The expansive surface provides plenty of space for the creative process. The neutral tone and texture of Homasote befit the studio cabin's natural setting.

2 BRING ADDITIONAL PURPOSE INTO A HALLWAY

While transforming a country home in Greenville, New York, design duo Tara Mangini and Percy Bright of Jersey Ice Cream Co covered a walkthrough hallway wall in Homasote and canvas. By doing so, they not only created a place for the owner to pin favourite maps and display treasured correspondence, they also transformed an under-utilised transitional area into a stopping place with purpose. The hallway now serves as an ever-evolving miniature gallery.

3 COVER HOMASOTE PANELS IN LINEN OR CANVAS

If the colour of raw Homasote boards does not suit an interior scheme, they can be transformed with a good latex paint in any colour. Another solution is to cover the panels in fabric. The heavier weave and tactile nature of linens and canvas are well-suited to industrial-style spaces. Athena Calderone, founder of EyeSwoon, made this trio of burlap-covered bulletin boards for her home office, fixing them to the wall using brass screws to complement the modern rustic look.

Michelberger Hotel

A CONVERTED TWENTIETH-CENTURY FACTORY WITH A LOW-KEY INDUSTRIAL LOOK

There is a youthful atmosphere and creative buzz about Berlin's Michelberger Hotel, housed in a former factory from 1903. The surrounding Friedrichshain district was formed around manufacturing and railway and water networks established during the late nineteenth century. Conveniently located for local transport links and beside the famous Oberbaum Bridge, the hotel is just a ten-minute walk from Berlin's Kreuzberg district and five minutes from the renowned East Side Gallery, the longest standing stretch of the Berlin Wall. Opened in 2009, Michelberger Hotel was originally designed by an in-house team in collaboration with the famous German furniture designer Werner Aisslinger. Danish architect Sigurd Larsen was responsible for the transformation of the lobby. London-based studio Jonathan Tuckey Design conceived an additional floor housing 23 new rooms.

Raw industrial features and creative twists in the independent hotel's revitalised interior spaces capture the spirit of the old factory and Germany's capital. The lobby, which channels a particularly urban vibe, has enormous timber and leather sofas, and this reception space has become a popular place to both work and socialise. The stylish adjoining café-bar opens early every morning for hotel guests and Berliners. There is also a large courtyard which doubles as a beer garden and concert venue. The atmosphere is informal. But while guests can expect a relaxed environment in the public spaces, the imaginatively styled guest rooms are tranquil retreats. The suites' open floor plates, beams and large windows create an understated industrial aesthetic, complemented by a neutral decorative palette and functional shapes. From the ground up, this is a truly individual boutique hotel and a great place to experience Berlin's creative spirit.

3.

1. In the new guest suites, conceived by British firm Jonathan Tuckey Design, the fine furniture, such as the beautiful beds, desks and benches, was also developed by the studio in Panzerholz. The sheet timber, formed under high pressure, secretes natural resins during manufacture for an aged look.

2. The enclosed areas have wooden palisaded frames. The form was inspired by the articulation of the S-Bahn signal box outside the hotel. It is an effective way to reference the locale and to create a dialogue between the interior spaces while playing with scale. Pale timber is a subtle industrial choice.

3. The Hideouts are self-contained suites placed at the front of the hotel. Each features a sauna, bath and shower in the bathroom. A connected layout and partitions with open panels maximise the sense of space and natural light. Bespoke shelving and the terrazzo floor tiles introduce a utilitarian edge.

4. Neutral tones in this guest bedroom create a calm and tranquil environment, with a welcoming king-size bed and smart desk area for those who need to work. Delicate terrazzo tiles in the open-plan bathroom provide the only patterning. This terrazzo is an attractive and light yet urban material.

4.

5. In the lobby, Sigurd Larsen hung chandeliers with clusters of amber-coloured spheres crafted by Berlin Art Glas. Beneath them, curvaceous sofas combine timber bases with comfortable leather cushions. The oversized wire-frame bookshelves filled with tomes emphasise the height of the space.

"We looked at some of the DDR-era architecture in the area for interior design inspiration."

SIGURD LARSEN

GET THE LOOK

TERRAZZO

Terrazzo is a colourful composite material combining marble, glass or quartz chippings, bound in cement or resin. It is both on-trend and timeless. There is an abundance of small accessories available, but large-scale terrazzo applications make the greatest impact.

1 TRANSFORM KITCHEN SURFACES WITH TERRAZZO

Marmoreal is an engineered marble terrazzo developed by Dzek in collaboration with British designer Max Lamb. It is available in two colourways, with either a white or black background. Each version comprises four Italian marbles, making up around 95 percent of the material. Tiles and slabs come in a variety of sizes, with polished or matt finishes. Marmoreal is an original alternative for kitchen counters and splashbacks, especially when it is fitted alongside brightly coloured cabinets.

2 JUXTAPOSE BATHROOM TILES WITH TERRAZZO

Terrazzo is a colourful and captivating alternative to concrete when remodelling a bathroom. Terrazzo Nouveau is a lovely porcelain tile by Mandarin Stone which mimics the appearance of real terrazzo. With a matt finish, it is suitable for use on floors as well as walls. Setting the cobalt Terrazzo Nouveau against Mandarin Stone's Norse midnight blue subway tiles creates a bold bathroom. Select brass elements are the perfect finishing touches for a sophisticated scheme.

3 TRY AN ALTERNATIVE TO TERRAZZO FLOORING

Foresso is a radical solution for sustainable interiors. Timber offcuts, mixed woodshavings and wood dust are combined and bound in resin to create a distinctive timber terrazzo. Natural oils and waxes give Foresso a durable finish, making it suitable for a range of applications including countertops. The Foresso floor tiles and planks are designed like terrazzo but manufactured like engineered timber, pre-finished with a tongue-and-groove base, making them easy to fit.

Armazém Luxury Housing

A FORMER METAL WAREHOUSE WITH TRANQUIL MODERN INDUSTRIAL INTERIORS

Set in a converted nineteenth-century iron warehouse, in the heart of the celebrated coastal city of Porto in northern Portugal, is a boutique hotel that is full of character. The second largest city in the country, Porto is also one of the oldest. In 1996, the historic centre was proclaimed a World Heritage Site by UNESCO. The Portuguese word for warehouse is Armazém and this hotel takes both its name as well as its interior style from the heritage of the building and the local area. Pedra Liquida, the Portuguese architecture studio responsible for the conversion of the former warehouse, intentionally retained all of the evidence of its industrial past. The materials palette for new additions was then carefully selected to complement those original features. The aim was also to highlight the duality of the property, as both a nineteenth-century warehouse building and a modern-day

hotel. Cold, raw materials are offset by warmer ones and soft surfaces. Bare stone walls, juxtaposed with polished concrete and aged metal, contrast with light timber. The result is an independent hotel filled with contemporary industrial character and imbued with a uniquely Portuguese modern rustic charm. A new iron staircase was inserted into the heart of the building to link the hotel's six floors, while also creating a strong focal point. There are nine different rooms in the principal warehouse hotel and three self-catering apartments in an adjacent building. The thoughtfully designed private apartments have mezzanine levels, which enhance the sense of light and space. They also offer private living rooms. All of the rooms are sparsely decorated and feel sophisticated and modern. Vibrant soft furnishings are used sparingly to add colour and a sense of homeliness to raw backdrops. This constant dialogue between old and new is dramatic and inviting.

1. The generously proportioned guest rooms have all been beautifully designed. Textured concrete on walls and ceilings displays the imprint of timber scaffold boards, enhancing the industrial look. A simple wooden bedhead complements the aesthetic.

2. The traditional woven rugs with vibrant geometric patterns add visual interest and splashes of colour to the otherwise unadorned guest suites. The minimal use of furniture feels modern, even while naked materials evoke the heritage of the warehouse.

3. In this spacious suite, a separate living area benefits from large glazed balcony doors and a high ceiling. The polished concrete floor reflects the natural light, making the space feel bright and airy. Velvet curtains and glass lanterns bring theatricality.

"Where iron was once stored, lasting memories are now created. The old warehouse has been reborn."

FERNANDA GRAMAXO, ARMAZÉM LUXURY HOUSING

4. There is a spacious terrace on which guests can enjoy a glass of port or wine with views over the city. For those staying in the penthouse, the romantic outlook across the rooftops of Porto is framed by a triangular window in the private attic living area.

5. The penthouse bedroom features a combined timber bed, headboard and storage unit. Stepped drawers, behind the bed, serve as a fun set of stairs, from the top of which guests can enjoy a peek through the skylight. It is an ingenious and unusual design.

TEXTURED CONCRETE

Concrete is the most widely used building material in the world. And it is particularly appropriate for industrial-inspired spaces. For those seeking an urban aesthetic, these innovative panels in various finishes make it easy to incorporate concrete into any interior.

USE CONCRETE PANELS TO CREATE TEXTURAL INTEREST

Multi-award-winning French brand Concrete LCDA specialises in fibre-reinforced concrete panels. This lightweight cladding, which is suitable for interior usage, combines a raw concrete surface with a foam backing. And once installed, the Panbeton panelling adopts the appearance of genuine concrete walls formed in situ. The panels are available in a wide variety of textured designs in light and dark tones. Concrete displaying the imprint of timber chipboard or scaffold boards will achieve a raw industrial backdrop, while a wood chevron effect in dark charcoal concrete will bring drama to any space. Easy to cut and install, Panbeton panels can be customised in line with a project and will transform rooms of any size. An ideal solution for designers and homeowners seeking a modern yet authentic urban look.

Ironworks Hotel Indy

A NEW HOTEL INSPIRED BY THE INDUSTRIAL HERITAGE OF AMERICA'S MIDWEST

L ocated on the north side of Indianapolis, Ironworks is a warehouse-style hotel completed in 2017. International design firm RATIO worked in close collaboration with real estate group Hendricks Commercial Properties to realise a new hotel with old-time character and charm. Architectural inspiration was drawn from the industrial heyday of America's Midwest, when factories were the pride and focus of local communities and things were built to last. The aim was also to create a destination for tourists and locals of Indiana alike that celebrated the unique culture of the state capital. And, while Ironworks Hotel Indy is filled with contemporary amenities, ranging from a modern fitness centre to a wide variety of restaurants, it seems its visitors are usually captivated by the nineteenth-century influences and heavy-duty industrial style of the interiors. The decorative schemes were

the responsibility of Garrett Cheyne, founder of Curate Design. Raw brick walls, weathered salvaged barn wood and iron, together with exposed pipes and metal ducting, establish a strong impression of an authentic industrial conversion. Every last detail has been carefully considered. Lights are suspended from pulleys in the lobby. Elevator graphics pay homage to factory workers of days gone by. The bell carts are fashioned from reclaimed piping. The 120 guest rooms range from the Traditional and Heritage rooms to the even larger Legacy and Founders suites, which boast private verandas with firepits. Brick walls, timber-clad ceilings and leather upholstery sit with quirky decorative touches, such as vintage hat moulds above the bedheads. Ironworks Hotel Indy was custom-built to honour the heavy industry referenced in its name. And it succeeds in providing memorable lodgings that guests are sorry to leave and eager to revisit.

1. The enormous American flag art installation displayed in the hotel lobby was created by visual artist Jim Spelman utilising old paper pattern moulds once used in manufacturing. It took hundreds of hours to format and bolt the parts in place and paint the work as the Star Spangled Banner.

2. Reclaimed timber flooring is used throughout the hotel. Salvaged wood also covers key architectural features, such as columns and archways. In the open two-level lobby, metal wall cladding offsets the wooden floor and acts as a backdrop to the staircase, which incorporates a boiler at its base.

3. A key benefit of this purpose-built hotel is the generous proportions of its guest rooms. While they are filled with industrial character, boasting soaring brick walls and expansive windows, there were none of the planning challenges that can arise in old factory or warehouse conversions.

4. The Founders Suite offers private dining for six beneath a large metal and glass chandelier suspended on chains. A partition wall, covered in reclaimed timber, separates the living and dining areas and contains a large television on both sides. Repurposed headlight covers now contain mirrors.

5. Floor-to-ceiling windows give the impression of an authentic factory while flooding the guest rooms and public spaces with natural light. Many of the guest suites include a Chesterfield leather sofa bed. A mid-century-style armchair and industrial coffee table complete this living area.

6. Salvaged barn wood, used for the floors throughout the hotel's public spaces, is inverted in the guest rooms and applied instead to the ceilings. Bare metal ductwork enhances the utilitarian look. A plush grey carpet suits the industrial-style features and steel blue walls but also adds softness.

RECLAIMED TIMBER

A sustainable solution for interiors, reclaimed timber also has a timeless quality that will never go out of style. Signs of wear enhance wood's character and form a material connection to the past. There are beautiful and surprising ways to use salvaged boards.

CONSIDER EVERY OPPORTUNITY TO UTILISE OLD WOOD

The owners of this 3,000 square foot property in London operate Encore Reclamation, a family business supplying reclaimed flooring and cladding, as well as vintage lighting, to homes and businesses around the world. When renovating their home in the famous Spratts dog biscuit factory, the couple drew on their extensive knowledge of salvaged materials and collaborated with Space Group Architects to create a residence that was suitable for the twenty-first century while honouring the industrial history of the Victorian building. The reclamation experts sourced quarter-sawn oak floorboards, previously laid in 1900 in London's Crosby Hall, and utilised these in every room, except for the bathrooms. Old ceiling joists were used to create the impression that the new first floor was original to the building. Reclaimed sapele hardwood was crafted into worktops atop modern moisture-resistant MDF kitchen cabinets. French railway carriage oak was found for a custom dining table. The juxtaposition of so many beautiful timbers and raw brick walls makes this a unique home and a popular photoshoot and film location.

2.

Paramount House Hotel

A FILM STUDIO HEADQUARTERS AND WAREHOUSE IN TRENDY SURRY HILLS

The old Paramount Pictures building is situated in Surry Hills, in the south-eastern corner of Sydney's Central Business District. Built in 1940 to house the film studio's commercial offices, the iconic Art Deco building is a well-known heritage site. But it had become dilapidated. Architecture practice Fox Johnston has been responsible for the steady transformation of the studio headquarters and its adjacent film warehouse since 2013. The project is a shining example of creative community collaborations. The Paramount Coffee Project and Golden Age Cinema and Bar opened in 2013, followed by the Paramount Recreation Centre and a co-working office space. In 2018, Paramount House Hotel was completed, occupying one full side of the building. A gilded crown, spanning and connecting the two buildings, is a nod to the golden age of cinema and enabled the

architects to establish a fourth floor atop the existing three storeys. A light-filled atrium marks the meeting point of the two buildings. The narrative of old and new continues throughout the interiors, which were undertaken by the Melbourne-based studio Breathe. The 27 rooms and two suites occupy the former film-storage warehouse. The bones of the old building remain, such as the original brick walls and evidence of patinated paint on their surfaces. These raw features are complemented by a robust palette of terrazzo bathroom tiles, copper pipes, architectural metalwork, reclaimed timber and concrete ceilings. Linen bedding, velvet upholstery and lush plants bring colour. The neighbourhood is one of Sydney's hippest, but it lacked a suitably trendy hotel until the opening of Paramount House. A concrete slab at the entrance to the boutique hotel reads 'Permanent Vacation'. Guests will be reluctant to leave these interiors.

4.

1. In the private living area of this Loft room, a blue Wilfred three-seater sofa and Alby ottoman, both by Australian furniture brand Jardan, invite guests to relax and unwind. For added cosiness, the floor is covered with a sumptuous carpet by Loom Rugs which features a colourful geometric pattern.

2. The hotel's beautiful new copper-clad rooftop extension serves two key purposes. The double-storey herringbone-patterned addition contributes visual drama to the buildings' exteriors, appearing as a crown on the original brick constructs. Inside, it provides screening for the interior guest balconies.

3. The guest rooms provide a lesson in material contrasts. Bare brick walls, concrete ceilings and timber floors are juxtaposed with terrazzo-lined bathrooms and bare copper pipes. Tactile indigo blankets by Seljak Brand, woven in Tasmania from recycled merino wool, complement linen bedding.

4. The beds are dressed in beautiful 100 percent pure European flax linen by Cultiver, which is stone-washed for softness. The 'dusk' and 'indigo' coloured bedding has proved so popular that it can be purchased in the hotel's online store. The hand-crafted mugs by Common Ceramics are sold too.

5. Every guest room has an individual identity and set of design details and the stylish bathrooms are also noteworthy. Some have a compact Japanese-style timber soaking tub, which is encircled by a linen shower curtain. The aged brass pipework shower rail and faucets add an industrial chic touch.

6. The serene and sophisticated bathrooms have terrazzo-tiled walls and terrazzo-topped wooden vanity units. Some feature charming sash windows in addition to exposed brick and concrete. The brown bottles of skin-care product by Australian brand Aesop suit the hotel aesthetic and ambience.

7. The herringbone-patterned trellis, which wraps around the top of the building, offers privacy for interior spaces while still allowing plenty of natural light. From this private veranda, guests can enjoy views through the copper lattice to the restored Griffiths Tea warehouse, converted into apartments.

> "We wanted to express everything about the existing warehouse that was old, authentic and raw, and capture the golden age of film."

JEREMY MCLEOD, BREATHE ARCHITECTURE

LINEN

While linen is similar to cotton, it is woven from flax which is tougher than cotton bolls. This makes linen more hard-wearing and gives it a rougher finish, which suits industrial schemes and spaces with raw architectural features. The appeal is practical and aesthetic.

1

SOURCE LINEN BED SHEETS IN A VIBRANT COLOUR
When dressing this relaxed bedroom scene, the Warehouse Home team chose Citrine bedding by LinenMe to offset the brown and orange tones of the reclaimed timber floorboards and the bare brick. A Mandarin linen throw from The Conran Shop completed the layering of the bed. A Lampe Gras table light with yellow shade by DCW éditions complements the linen. It stands on a classic metal Nicolle chair, a sturdy metal factory stool which has been in production since 1913.

2

PAIR LINEN BEDDING WITH LUXURIOUS VELVET
The success of this beautiful bedroom scheme by Warehouse Home rests upon the textural contrast between the bed and the bedding. The Raul kingsize bed from Barker and Stonehouse is upholstered in sumptuous Old Rose velvet. Our team selected linen pillowcases in both Salmon and Raw Umber from Larusi in London. The linen duvet cover in Rusty Orange is by Italian brand Society Limonta. The pale pink wool blanket, also by Society Limonta, adds further texture.

3

SELECT PASTEL SHADES TO COMPLEMENT RAW PLASTERWORK FOR A LIGHT INDUSTRIAL LOOK
London-based brand LinenMe is a family business committed to the sustainable production of linen homeware and clothes that suit a pared-back lifestyle. This lovely bedroom setting is characterised by a bare plaster wall. The Rosa linen duvet cover is pre-washed for extra softness and does not need to be ironed, making it both practical and pretty. The delicate crumpling suits the soft industrial aesthetic.

4

ADD VISUAL INTEREST WITH A SUBTLE STRIPE
The Sid stripe bedding set from Secret Linen Store features a tiny French blue line detail woven into the off-white 100 percent linen fabric. The pillowcases have a small border as an additional, but unfussy, detail. Washed and tumbled, the sheets and covers have a relaxed appearance. The understated design is equally well-suited to a coastal retreat, quaint country cottage or warehouse home, but looks especially striking against this two-tone painted brick wall.

Soho House Chicago

A HIP AND HAPPENING HUB IN A CONVERTED BELT FACTORY

When Soho House Chicago opened in August 2014, it was the fourth American outpost for the London-based private members club founded for those in the creative industries. It is situated in the Allis Building, in the Fulton Market District. Built in 1907, the building originally housed the Chicago Belting Company, a leather tannery. It would later become a factory making rubber sealants. Chicago-based firm Hartshorne Plunkard Architecture, working with the Soho House design team, oversaw the conversion of the former industrial building and preserved as many existing materials as possible. Among the key structures that were retained was a sizeable board-formed concrete structure, which is now the highlight of the lobby. Existing steel windows were deemed to be beyond repair, but were replaced with modern alternatives that still maintained the distinctive historical detailing of the building. Soho House Chicago has the atmosphere and aesthetic of a bohemian artist's loft. Modern works on display include pieces by Damien Hirst and local creatives. There are plenty of perks available to the boutique hotel's non-member guests. Meanwhile, for members there is a rooftop pool and a brick-walled gym with boxing ring. The 40 guest rooms, available to Soho House members and Soho friends, honour the building's history in their design. Their high ceilings and reclaimed timber floors are balanced by custom-made wallpaper, vintage radiators and handcrafted carpets or rugs. Dark leather and velvet upholstered furniture completes the sophisticated schemes, while rotary telephones and glass mini-bars add to the vintage-style charm. Whether dropping in to work and socialise or staying longer to relax, every visitor appreciates ultra-stylish Soho House Chicago.

3.

1. The ground-floor Allis bar and lounge is named after the family that originally commissioned the historic belt factory building. Its dramatic proportions and impressive display of artworks make it an appealing spot for coffee meetings and informal drinks. The mezzanine level, now the Allis lounge, is where workers once tanned the hides used for belt making.

2. The Club Bar is situated on the fifth floor. At its centre is a reclaimed oval bar encircled by stools that have been upholstered in deep red velvet. The ceiling, clad in salvaged tin tiles, is softly lit by crystal orb pendants. Table lamps around the bar also offer gentle illumination and an intimate ambience befitting one of the city's most desirable evening hang-out spots.

3. The Drawing Room is welcoming and comfortable. It is an expansive open-plan environment, but it has been cleverly divided into intimate seating areas that suit meetings and relaxation alike. During the day, ping pong tables double as work tables. Bare brick and exposed concrete are offset by parquet flooring, vintage-style seating upholstered in leather and velvet, and glistening chandeliers.

4. Of the 40 smart guest rooms, no two are alike. Again, the building's heritage features informed the design process. The Soho House design team, led by resident designer Vicky Charles and group owner Nick Jones, sourced unique furnishings from all over the world, weaving together a variety of interior styles. In this suite, a traditional four-poster frames the view from the bed of the raw concrete ceiling, illuminated by a delicate chandelier. It is complemented by the reclaimed hardwood floors, mirrored side units and seating upholstered in velvet.

"The renovation restored unique features of the old building. Period details include vintage tiles and a lobby wall clad in wood from the original rooftop water tower."

HARTSHORNE PLUNKARD
ARCHITECTURE

4.

GET THE LOOK

VELVET

Touches of velvet transform an interior scheme from raw industrial to sophisticated and luxurious. The sumptuous textural qualities of velvet make a striking impression against bare brickwork or concrete. Jewel tones and rich colours add warmth and visual contrast.

1 ENJOY CHIC DESIGNS CREATED FOR TOP HOTELS

Soho Home is an interiors collection for Soho House that includes furniture, lighting and decorative accessories created for, as well as inspired by, the brand's outposts around the world. For any guests hoping to mirror the look and feel of Soho House Chicago, there are several velvet-upholstered items, including sofas and armchairs, that can be made to order. The Manette bedstead in super-fine velvet brings Soho House chic to the bedroom and is particularly striking in navy. It is modelled on beds at Kettner's in London and certainly suggests long lie-ins.

3 CHOOSE TEALS FOR VINTAGE-STYLE INTERIORS

Warehouse Home picked sofa.com's two-seat Zeppelin design in deep turquoise velvet for this Victorian warehouse conversion. The mid-century form with tapered wooden legs and buttoned back suited the heritage space. The colour and velvet upholstery were timeless. The sofa stood on an Artwork 3 carpet by Jan Kath for Krassky, selected for its lightly aged look. Vintage-style accessories, including a lovely handmade globe by Bellerby & Co, enhanced the space's old-world charm.

2 LAYER UP ON LUXURIOUS VELVET ACCESSORIES

In this atmospheric bedroom scene, conceived by Warehouse Home, the brass Alana bed from Made stands against a bare brick wall. To create a sophisticated 'industrial luxe' scheme, the bed is dressed in midnight blue. Propped against the head is an array of cushions in opulent velvets and silks woven with metallics. A velvet linen throw by Niki Jones brings further richness. The illuminated table, upcycled from a water boiler by Rockit Home, adds a quirky industrial edge.

4 SELECT PALE GREYS TO COMPLEMENT METALS

Acro- wallpaper in blue and silver is the result of an exclusive collaboration between Warehouse Home and 17 Patterns. The design was inspired by the surface corrosion of metal. To complement the digitally crafted patina on the walls, and a sizeable steel column in this factory home, the team sourced the Iggy chaise from sofa.com in 'Squirrel' grey. Alongside it are a handcrafted metal table by The Rag And Bone Man and accessories in spun and hammered brass.

The Warehouse Hotel

A BOUTIQUE HOTEL THAT UNLOCKS THE UNIQUE QUALITIES OF A SINGAPOREAN ICON

Sitting alongside the Singapore River is an old warehouse with a fascinating history. Built in 1895, on what was once a busy and important trade route, the 'godown' (or warehouse) originally stored exotic spices at the height of Singapore's spice trade. Robertson Quay was then a hotbed of underground activity and liquor distilleries. Years later, in the 1980s, the colonial-era spice warehouse housed a disco. Later still, it was used as an oil mill. The local architecture studio Zarch Collaboratives, together with the branding and interior design firm Asylum collaborated on the transformation of the heritage building into a boutique hotel. Careful attention has been paid throughout the conversion to preserving and celebrating as many of the original features as possible, while introducing new design details inside that honour local culture and heritage. The louvre windows, the doors,

the cornices and mouldings were all sensitively restored. A double-volume hotel lobby greets guests upon their arrival. A black metal gate and bare brick wall have been retained. Enormous refurbished trusses spanning the space have been painted black and highlighted by a dramatic installation of industrial parts. Throughout this space, and the hotel as a whole, materials were selected to reference the building's past while also bringing warmth and comfort. Brown leather furniture features prominently in the lobby. Metal frames and mid-century inspired forms suit the contemporary industrial look. The mixed aesthetic continues in the guest accommodation. Black ceiling trusses are exposed here too, while the metal-framed furniture accommodates timber and marble cabinets for wardrobes, desks and wash basins. Guests will find every contemporary luxury in this century-old warehouse conversion in a very modern city-state.

1. The modern interiors incorporate industrial textures with luxe finishes. Supple leather features prominently in the hotel lobby, where it covers seats from Jess Design and Stellar Works that invite all guests to unwind.

2. The former warehouse combines a trio of gabled, connected buildings. Following a two-year renovation, it has been successfully reimagined as a boutique hotel that is as distinctive as the sovereign island city-state itself.

3. An installation of wheels, cogs and pulleys is suspended above the hotel's lobby. It is a reminder of the historic building's industrial past and at the same time emphasises the dramatic proportions of the hotel entrance hall.

"The hotel provides an account of Singapore's developing days where economic and underground activities flourished as a trading port."

CHRIS LEE, ASYLUM

3.

4.

4. & 5. The boutique hotel's 37 loft-style guest suites are minimalist in design. Black metal-framed contemporary furniture and structural features suit the heritage of the building and call to mind the enormous original trusses that impress guests upon their arrival in the hotel lobby. Glazed and open frameworks separate the bedrooms and bathrooms while retaining chic open-plan living arrangements.

GET THE LOOK

LEATHER

Leather is ideally suited to industrial conversions and utilitarian schemes. Durable and flexible and available in a wide range of modern colours and finishes, as well as natural tones and textures, it can be formed into unusual shapes, studded, stitched and more.

1 INVEST IN BEAUTIFUL MODERN LEATHER SEATING
Overgaard & Dyrman is a contemporary furniture-design studio based in Denmark. The brand combines traditional techniques with modern technology to create handcrafted pieces that connect the past with the present. The Wire Collection, which includes the Wire Lounge Sofa, showcases the time-honoured crafts of saddle-making and metalwork. Each item is numbered and stamped with the initials of the skilled craftsperson who made the individual steel and leather components.

2 SEEK SINUOUS AND SURPRISING APPLICATIONS
The Fred desk from Poltrona Frau features a single piece of saddle leather specially treated to curve and flow over the front of the solid ash-framed desk and elegantly conceal the wooden drawer. There are no stitches or seams, the raw edge of the leather is simply finished with protective wax. Delicate carvings and cold markings create fine graphic decorations on the leather's surface. Fred is a unique modern interpretation of the traditional leather-topped writing desk.

3 **INCLUDE LEATHER FOR A SMARTER BEDROOM**
Danish design company BY THORNAM has released The M, a multifunctional item of leather furniture that can be used as a futon, daybed, lounge chair or headboard. As a headboard, it can be mounted from its leather loops using rings or from a bar. Founder Mads Thornam was originally inspired by a 1930s leather gym mat he found in an antique store in Copenhagen. Leather ages over time, which means The M develops an authentic patina and homely appearance.

5 **FIND DISTINCTIVE LEATHER LIGHTING DESIGNS**
Lighting is a stylish and surprising way to incorporate leather into an interior scheme. The HangUp wall lamp (above) by Ted Jefferis combines British saddle leather, English Oak and solid brass. The leather shade develops a beautiful patina with age and emits a warm glow. Warehouse Home suspended a Long John pendant light from a beamed ceiling to create this atmospheric dining space (below). Made in Scandinavia, it comes with brass spotlights and simple leather straps.

4 **LOOK FOR STUDDING AND OTHER DETAILING**
Celebrated furniture and homeware designer Bethan Gray describes her work as storytelling through craft and design. The Siena collection was inspired by Gray's travels through Europe and includes a series of leather tables. The Brogue tables are trimmed with perforated belting leather, which is laser cut with a delicate pattern reminiscent of traditional broguing on shoes. The Stud leather tables were inspired by a Medieval studded door in Siena cathedral.

Ace Hotel Chicago

A CONVERTED CHEESE-MAKING FACTORY SHOWING BAUHAUS INFLUENCES

L ifestyle hotel brand Ace has a number of outposts, in the UK, America and Japan. This was Commune Design studio co-founder Roman Alonso's fourth collaboration with the group. But Ace Hotel Chicago was the brand's first ground-up property and offered a set of interesting challenges as a result, mainly due to the lack of historic architecture on site. The old brick façade on part of the building, which was once home to a cheese-making factory, was painstakingly restored and a new addition made inspired by the Bauhaus philosophy, established in Chicago in 1937. Inside, Alonso drew plenty of inspiration from Chicago's rich design heritage and was particularly guided by the iconic work of American architect Ludwig Mies van der Rohe, who practiced in downtown Chicago for over 30 years. Simple materials thoughtfully combined evoke Mies van der Rohe's achievements at the Illinois Institute of Technology. The architect had an affinity for wood panelling for example; plywood panels appear throughout the hotel. Clean lines define the public spaces and guest rooms. And in many places, mid-western craftsmanship merges in with utilitarian design to great effect. Much of the furniture shows a strong mid-century influence, reminiscent of designs originally conceived in the 1930s at the Bauhaus school, where Mies van der Rohe acted as its last director. Linoleum and polished steel reference the creations of renowned modernists Arne Jacobsen and Richard Neutra too. And pops of blue, green, pink and yellow add a contemporary twist. Each guest room features a unique piece of art from a student at School of the Art Institute of Chicago. Ace Hotel's interior spaces offer the essence of New Bauhaus style in Chicago and a lesson in channelling industrial style combined with mid-century modern flair.

1. In the Little Wild rooftop bar, black terrazzo floor tiles inject industrial style from the ground up. Plywood panels on the walls and ceiling are a nod to Mies van der Rohe's love of wood panelling, but have been given a contemporary makeover in black.

2. The bar features a DJ booth constructed from giant sand wall blocks, an ideal accompaniment to the space's thick-set concrete pillars. Meanwhile, the understated blue and grey palette complements the bar's panoramic views of the Chicago skyline.

3. Folded metal shelving, powder-coated in pale green, provides visual interest in this bathroom by contrasting with the deep blue square tiles and ply panels. The tubular frame supporting the basin conveniently doubles as hanging space for towels.

4. Factory window-style shower screens reinforce the bathroom's urban aesthetic. The square panes also mimic the square wall tiles. The thicker black frames make a powerful style statement when offset against the blue floor and walls in a compact space.

3.

4.

5. Exposed concrete ceilings set the tone for bold industrial interiors, supported by plywood desks that run full-width beneath the bedroom windows. Denim-upholstered chairs and headboards inlaid with blue linoleum add colour and utilitarian chic.

6. Chrome tubing is a design reference to Bauhaus and enhances the industrial character of this guest room as it is also reminiscent of exposed pipework. The bespoke tubing rack frames the wall-mounted television and has hooks to hold guests' belongings.

5.

TUBULAR STEEL

For over 100 years, tubular steel has enabled radical furniture designs, from pieces that stack to items that can be reconfigured endlessly in line with changing requirements. Resembling exposed piping, cylindrical metal tube frameworks suit any industrial scheme.

1 USE ICONIC TUBULAR-STEEL FURNITURE DESIGNS

Marcel Breuer was still an apprentice at the Bauhaus when, in 1925, he designed the Model B3 or Wassily Chair. Reimagining the classic club chair, Breuer was inspired by the thin metal frame of a bicycle and influenced by the pared-back aesthetic and geometric forms of the De Stijl movement. His chair's elemental form, in tubular steel, was fabricated using plumbing techniques. It changed the course of furniture design forever and the chair is still produced to this day, by Knoll.

2 CUSTOMISE A TUBULAR-STEEL-FRAMED DESIGN WITH COLOURFUL POWDER-COATED ADDITIONS

Renowned Swiss brand USM is the leading name in modular furniture. The patented USM ball joint connects frameworks built in square and rectangular formats. These units can then be continually modified and extended. Powder-coated steel panels, doors and drawers, available in 14 different colours, combine with the chrome-plated tubular-steel frames to complete vibrant furniture to suit any home and room.

3 TRANSFORM A ROOM DIVIDER WITH LIGHTING

The USM Modular Furniture configurator tool enables users to create their own designs from scratch. One of the elements that can be added to a customised piece is the innovative Haller E system. The discrete and streamlined lighting solution is built into USM furniture's tubular-steel framework. When switched off, it is virtually invisible. But switched on, light gently illuminates the unit. Haller E is particularly striking when incorporated into a room-divider unit.

Locke At Broken Wharf

A RIVERSIDE OFFICE BLOCK CONVERTED INTO AN URBAN HIDEAWAY

Located on the north bank of the River Thames, Locke At Broken Wharf is a stylish new apartment hotel. It is within walking distance of many of London's cultural hotspots. St Paul's Cathedral is just a short amble from the hotel. The world-famous Tate Modern gallery, Shakespeare's Globe theatre and the many restaurants and coffee shops along the South Bank, are all a comfortable stroll away on the other side of the river. The hotel occupies a seven-storey 1970s office block, which needed to be completely gutted and remodelled. New York-based architecture firm Grzywinski+Pons was responsible for the transformation. For the interiors, the studio drew inspiration from the dichotomy of the British capital's cityscape. There is plenty of urban grit, as well as softer textures and tones chosen to reflect the serenity of the Thames. In the public spaces, which include a bar, deli-style all-day restaurant and a vibrant co-working space, ducting and pipework have been left exposed for a raw industrial look. Wire-mesh furniture and accessories further enhance the aesthetic. The grittier features are softened by butterscotch paint. Terrazzo floors, light timber and textural contrasts introduced by leather sofas and rattan lights, complete a scheme that is both cool and contemporary. The 113 spacious riverside studios also combine pastel shades, pale wood and marble, offset by touches of brass and colourful wire mesh, which establishes a modern yet serene environment for leisure and business guests alike. The largest guest rooms, Locke Studios and River Suites, are ideally suited for longer stays, with separate sleeping and living areas and well-equipped kitchens. It is clear that Locke At Broken Wharf was thoughtfully designed for travellers looking for more than just a bed for the night in Britain's busy capital.

1. The apartment hotel offers many lessons in the use of contrasting materials in interior design. In the larger suites, the plywood kitchen cabinetry is balanced by marble countertops and splashbacks. The lighter tones suit the pastel green of the walls.

2. Guests at Locke At Broken Wharf enjoy direct vistas of Tate Modern. The world-famous modern art gallery, as well as the popular restaurants and theatres of London's lively South Bank, are just a five-minute walk away, over the Millennium Bridge.

3. The use of space has been carefully considered. A piping hanging rail cleverly incorporates a small circular bedside shelf. A deeper headboard creates an area to display artwork and ornaments. A pair of glass and brass pendant lights illuminates the bed.

4. A coffee table with pink wire-mesh base and a marble top takes centre stage in this living area. The hanging rail serves as a room divider while retaining a loft-style open-plan living arrangement and ensuring the super views can always be enjoyed.

3.

4.

5.

5. The design-led co-working area is a welcoming environment, where artisanal coffee can be enjoyed by day and cocktails savoured at night. Pastel tones effectively soften the urban aesthetic created by the exposed ducting and structural steel. Industrial in style, it is also a calm and relaxed setting for both independent work and group meetings. There are separate seats for those seeking space to focus and large comfortable sofas for socialising with others.

"Perforated
stainless steel
panels and chain
mail curtains
contrast with green
onyx, suede, leather,
wool and tweed
upholstery, timber,
jute, rattan,
creamy terrazzo
and limestone."

GRZYWINSKI+PONS

COLOURED WIRE

Wire mesh is increasingly being utilised in interior design schemes. Galvanised metal is ideal for an industrial aesthetic. But mesh powder-coated in a vibrant colour, whether used in large or small volumes, offers the opportunity to give any project a modern twist.

1 USE COLOURED MESH PANELS TO PRESERVE AND SHOWCASE EXISTING ARCHITECTURAL FEATURES

When OTTOTTO studio removed the old plaster from this house in Porto, Portugal, they uncovered two imposing stone walls. The architects selected metallic mesh panels to protect the building's heritage and highlight this original stonework. The light green tone of the wire is a link to the green floor and painted beams. The wire mesh also serves as a material connection to the thin steel used to create the staircase.

2

MIX AND MATCH COLOURFUL WIRE HOMEWARE
(Clockwise from right) Beijing-based People's Industrial Design Office conceived the minimalist Mesh Chair to be crafted from a single metal rod. Large gaps left in the diagonal pattern, where support is not required, reduce the amount of material used. The Panton Wire System, released in 1971 and available today from Montana Furniture, is at once raw and industrial, elegant and timeless. The Net Side Table, designed by Benjamin Hubert for Moroso, is manufactured from laser-cut carbon steel and is available in a range of colours. It appears light or solid depending on the viewer's position. The Twiggy Grid LED suspension light by Foscarini can be utilised in exterior and interior settings.

Colour

There is a common misconception that an authentic industrial interior must be monochromatic. A utilitarian scheme certainly looks dramatic when incorporating variations of grey or black. Pale greys complement and mimic the tones of raw concrete, while charcoal décor can offset structural steels or metal-framed furniture for a heavy-duty look. But there are actually a number of ways to incorporate colour into heritage conversions and industrial-inspired spaces. Shades might be soft and subtle, warm or vibrant. There might be a single accent colour, complementary pairs or clashing combinations. Painting constructional features, such as columns or trusses, will immediately call attention to these elements and give a historic building a contemporary twist. Colour can also be successfully introduced through furniture and decorative lighting choices, as well as high-impact wall treatments. When it comes to colour in industrial interiors, there is a whole spectrum of opportunity.

The cavernous lobby of Stamba Hotel in Tbilisi, Georgia, still retains many of its original structures. The hotel is housed in the former headquarters of a Soviet printing house and, fittingly, this reception hall is encircled by bookshelves. The spines of the tomes inject an array of colours into the space. Large portions of the exposed concrete were painted a rich teal, drawing attention to the textural quality and adding drama.

2.

Fabriken Furillen

A FORMER LIMESTONE REFINERY IN A CINEMATIC SETTING

The landscape of Furillen peninsula, in the north east of the Swedish island Gotland, is wild and untamed. The area is famous for its natural beauty, characterised by a rugged coastline and windswept pines. But it has also gained renown for the privately owned boutique hotel located there. Fabriken Furillen is a former limestone refinery which has been converted into a unique eco hotel. The deserted factory, adopted by the military since 1974, was discovered in the 1990s by entrepreneur and photographer Johan Hellström while he was scouting for photo shoot locations. Hellström chose to preserve the original industrial infrastructure, such as the old workers' canteen. Reclaimed regional materials, including hardwood, limestone and concrete, were used in the construction of the 18 guest rooms, which stand separate from the main building. But while there is a material richness to the accommodation, the rooms are actually sparingly decorated, minimalist retreats. White-washed walls maximise the natural light and the sense of calm. The clean lines of the essential items of furniture and a complete lack of decorative clutter ensures guests are able to savour the peacefulness and views without any distraction. The rooms encapsulate Swedish minimalism with a few subtle industrial touches, such as the utilitarian lighting. They prove that less really can be more in design. For those seeking absolute off-the-grid escapism hermit huts, situated further out in the wilderness and lacking electricity and running water, offer an even more remote experience. This almost other-worldly site has long been a popular location for filming and photo shoots. Now, with the conversion of Fabriken Furillen into an exceptional small hotel, visitors come in search of the interiors inspiration it provides as much as the isolation.

1. Full-height steel-framed windows reinforce the industrial character of Fabriken Furillen and form a dramatic backdrop to the open-air dining tables. The hotel's dramatic surroundings, both natural and quarried, are reflected in the square glass panes.

2. The simplicity of Fabriken Furillen's structure ensures that the hotel's remarkable environment dominates guests' experiences. Juxtaposed with the lunar appearance of the abandoned quarry are the untamed rocky coastline and glistening sea beyond.

3. Sizeable areas of floor-to-ceiling glass brickwork flood the boutique hotel's communal areas with natural light. This glazing also complements the factory-style doors and effectively underscores the attractive Scandinavian-meets-industrial aesthetic.

4. A simple metal log burner complements the chic industrial interior style as much as it suits the cold Swedish winters. It also creates an attractive focal point for an informal seating area, with a selection of comfortable armchairs upholstered in grey felt.

5. Exposed structural steels, and pulleys and chains suspended from the ceiling, evoke the old factory workers' canteen and remind guests of Fabriken Furillen's industrial past. Minimal décor, with pale timber and shades of grey, complements bare metal.

6. The sparse and considered decoration of the guest rooms enhances the sense of calm. Every item serves a clear purpose. Pale timber flooring and selected white elements feature sparingly in the rooms' monochromatic schemes in grey shades.

7. Wool blankets and sheepskin rugs add textural interest to the simplistic spaces. The grid print on the guest bedding is a subtle link to the square panels of the factory-style windows. The views are so captivating that no televisions are needed.

SHADES OF GREY

Grey has long been associated with heavy-duty industrial materials and settings. As a result, it can be feared a drab choice for interiors. But layering this elegant neutral creates refined schemes that complement any heritage features and also suit modern-day living.

DRAW ON THE COOL TONES OF STRUCTURAL STEELS AND ESTABLISH A SOPHISTICATED GREY INTERIORS PALETTE

This top-floor apartment in Cape Town, South Africa, is the home of Kim Smith, an interior designer and the director of furniture and homewares store Weylandts. Renovating the loft in 2017, Smith took the opportunity to introduce a strong industrial aesthetic. Structural steels, left uncovered, now frame the interior spaces, while exposed brickwork has been painted Aniseed grey to create a dark and moody backdrop. Dark-stained oak flooring and concrete floor tiles were introduced, together with a large granite island. Tempering this utilitarian background, Smith has layered further shades of grey and selected furnishings in a variety of rich textures. A number of items were sourced, of course, from Weylandts. Floor-to-ceiling windows provide plenty of natural light throughout the property, but the grey palette contrasts with the bright outside world to create a soothing cocooning effect.

1.

2.

The Krane

AN UNCONVENTIONAL ONE-ROOM HOTEL IN COPENHAGEN

Standing majestically at the entrance of Nordhavn in Copenhagen is a unique and immersive single-bedroom hotel. A former coal crane, originally constructed in 1944, has been converted into a unique private retreat for two adults, with a spa and sauna and a meeting space. Towering 15 metres over the harbourside, the steel crane has undergone an inspirational remodel, thanks to the vision of owner Klaus Kastbjerg and Copenhagen architecture firm Arcgency. To pay homage to the history of the industrial structure, the interiors are predominantly a deep, coal black. The decorative treatments also reflect several key Danish design ideologies: modern furniture, decluttered space and a 'less is more' approach. In order to maintain the minimalist ambience, the simple furniture has been custom-made to ensure the pieces can disappear into integrated wall panels.

The effect is uniquely calming and aesthetically impactful. The dark interiors dramatically frame the harbour views while creating a sense of retreating from the world outside. On closer inspection, the minimalist interiors have a rich textural quality. Wood, leather, stone and steel make up the majority of the materials used for the décor. It is a typically Scandinavian approach to interior design, yet it is also a treatment that suits this industrial conversion as the natural elements effectively offset the undisguised heavy-duty construction details. Klaus Kastbjerg has a passion for the preservation of former industrial buildings and has purchased several properties around Copenhagen since the 1980s. The Silo is a decommissioned grain depository he successfully converted for housing in 2017. But The Krane demonstrates that even former industrial machinery can be salvaged for an entirely new purpose. It is an architectural triumph.

1. The Krane offers tranquil spaces for rest and reflection. Unnecessary elements have been excluded from the interiors and the walls are bare, ensuring that the spectacular views serve as living art and the blackened timbers create strong viewing frames.

2. The impressive steel structure is set at the edge of the harbour and offers guests panoramic views of the waterfront, the city of Copenhagen and the sea beyond from every level. The boardroom, encircled in glass, is a dramatic setting for any meeting.

3. At the top of the decommissioned crane, the former engine room now houses the contemporary bedroom. From the timber floors and in-built joinery to the custom-built furniture in polished stone and leather, the calm area combines many shades of black.

4. A spa, created within a shipping container, is clad in light grey stone tiles. A pair of elegant bathtubs, set side by side, offer another vantage point from which to enjoy the vistas. The wall-to-wall glazing also enables guests to admire the structural steels.

5. The Danish flooring firm Dinesen treated the Douglas fir floor and wall timbers with a specially formulated colour called 'megablack'. Integrated storage dissolves into wood panelling and maximises the sense of space while preserving the spartan aesthetic.

6. Copenhagen is widely regarded as the style capital of Scandinavia. And The Krane is certainly the Danish capital's most unusual, if not also its coolest, hotel concept. It embraces its industrial locale and heritage while offering a uniquely memorable stay.

BLACK

Black is a dramatic choice for the home. Bold homeowners might paint feature walls or whole rooms. But even in smaller doses, black is sharp and sophisticated, defining specific focal points and functional areas through stark contrast with lighter and brighter spaces.

CREATE EXCITING VARIATIONS BETWEEN LIGHTER AND DARKER INTERIOR SPACES AND INCORPORATE TEXTURE

This unusual loft, in downtown Seattle's historic Pioneer Square, provides valuable lessons in the use of tonal and textural contrasts in interior design. The apartment was designed by Plum Projects and Corey Kingston (now running her own studio, Le Whit). The New York-based client, working in the tech industry, was seeking a relaxing pied-à-terre and incubator space in his hometown of Seattle. To keep an open-plan format, Kingston designed a mezzanine bedroom above an L-shaped wrap-around unit which houses a washroom, shower, toilet and sauna. The four bathroom compartments are clad entirely in Shou Sugi Ban (charred timber which is resistant to mould) and have black cement floor tiles. In the living area, brick walls and ducting are painted white and white kitchen cabinets are paired with white wall tiles. Light and dark reinforce the transition between spaces and functions.

2.

Titanic Hotel

A CONVERTED RUM WAREHOUSE IN A HISTORIC PORT

Stanley Dock is one of the most recognisable areas of Liverpool, a former industrial powerhouse in the north of England. Once part of the Port of Liverpool, and now a UNESCO World Heritage Site, the dock has been significantly transformed over recent years and it continues to be sensitively redeveloped. Standing in the heart of this historic setting, Titanic Hotel is housed within a preserved Victorian warehouse that was once used to store rum. Family-owned Irish property company Harcourt Developments adopted a considered approach to the conversion, working with heritage consultant John Hinchliffe and Darmody Architecture to preserve and celebrate the listed warehouse shell. The award-winning interior designers ADI Studio introduced decorative solutions that retained the dramatic proportions of the heritage building while also creating a sense of comfort and intimacy. The contemporary décor has been sensitively selected to suit the enormous spaces and raw industrial features. Even seasoned travellers will be impressed by the size of the guest rooms. In the public areas, the cool stone flooring, metal-framed furniture and reclaimed timber salvaged on site all complement the exposed brickwork and towering cast iron columns. The leather and velvet upholstery adds further textural interest. The choice of a muted colour palette throughout the hotel ensures the focus remains on the magnitude of the nineteenth-century warehouse and its views of the historic port. The remarkable transformation has brought new life to Stanley Dock's North warehouse, but preserved the charm of the original Victorian architecture. There is no better place to soak up the rich history and atmosphere of Liverpool, but Titanic Hotel has become a travel destination in its own right too.

1. Stanley's Bar and Grill at Titanic Hotel has been likened to a theatre for dining. In addition to its soaring steel columns, its waterfront setting gives dramatic views of Stanley Dock.

2. Titanic Hotel is situated in what was once the largest, most complete system of historic docks in the world. It faces a converted Victorian tobacco warehouse, now luxury apartments.

3. Every one of the 153 beautifully appointed rooms features warehouse windows. Many also boast dramatic brick-vaulted ceilings. Neutral décor ensures such features are the key focus.

4. The light grey metro tiles in the well-appointed and spacious guest bathrooms evoke the exposed brick walls found throughout the hotel. The look is contemporary yet timeless.

5. The hotel's spa is a subterranean sanctuary, with a hydrotherapy pool, relaxation loungers and ten tranquil treatment rooms all set beneath the brick arches of the former warehouse.

NEUTRALS

A neutral palette offers many benefits. In a heritage property, it ensures the emphasis remains on original features such as exposed brick and old timbers. In any home, a lack of strong colour creates a sense of spaciousness and serenity and enhances natural light.

A NEUTRAL SCHEME ENHANCES A COMPACT APARTMENT

This loft apartment is situated in a former marmalade factory complex in Szczecin, Poland, and was originally used as a warehouse storage space. Local interior design studio Loft Kolasinski kept many of the property's original features, including its high brick barrel-vaulted ceilings and large arched windows. The old wooden floors were also retained and restored. In order to enhance the natural light in the apartment, a minimalist scheme and neutral colour palette were employed. In the open-plan living room, a kitchenette runs along the full length of one wall. Comprising plywood base units, with no wall cupboards and a white marble countertop, it has an understated appearance. A lightly coloured 1930s Polish rug complements the pale plywood cabinets. The calm yet characterful scheme is completed with light brown leather upholstery and assorted 1950s and 1960s wooden furniture from Poland, the Czech Republic, Denmark and the Netherlands.

1.

2/

Lokal

LAID BACK STYLE WITH INDUSTRIAL INFLUENCES IN PHILADELPHIA

This beautifully designed boutique hotel is located in the heart of Philadelphia's Old City. It is set in a brick-built nineteenth-century property which previously housed a printworks. On its doorstep are quaint tree-lined streets, heritage sites, boutique shops, cafés, bars and galleries. Lokal founders Chad and Courtney Ludeman wanted to create a memorable home-from-home experience for short- and long-term guests. They enlisted the interior design services of Tara Mangini and Percy Bright of Jersey Ice Cream Co to help them realise their vision. Each of the six one- and two-bedroom loft apartment-style suites is filled with natural light and offers a comfortable living area as well as a fully-equipped and stylish kitchen. The Jersey Ice Cream Co duo stuck to their favourite materials palette of plaster, concrete, leather, linen, timber and brass. And they opted for a largely neutral scheme with just a single rich accent colour, blue. The raw plaster walls (a signature treatment from Tara and Percy) complement the building's features and light-industrial past while also achieving an understated, modern aesthetic. Furnishings were sourced from well-known homeware brands such as Crate & Barrel, CB2, Article, Casper and Parachute because Lokal's owners wanted guests to be able to purchase items they admired during their stays. But the suites feature a healthy mixture of vintage furniture and custom-made pieces too. The bathroom vanity units, kitchen cabinets and sealed concrete countertops were all created by local craftspeople. Each of Lokal's rooms has a guide to the neighbourhood's sights, shops and eateries. But the real appeal of staying at this distinctive hotel is that it offers, as its name suggests, the opportunity to enjoy Philadelphia as a resident. A resident with a particularly well-designed home that is.

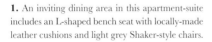

1. An inviting dining area in this apartment-suite includes an L-shaped bench seat with locally-made leather cushions and light grey Shaker-style chairs.

2. Brass hardware and light fittings and concrete countertops complete the kitchenettes, which are painted in Sherwin-Williams' bold Seaworthy blue.

3. In this bathroom, a large concrete basin sits on a sturdy timber base. Simple glossy white metro tiles provide a textural contrast with the basin unit.

4. This interior warehouse window with textured glass echoes the building's original fenestration and is an attractive way to partition an open-plan suite.

BLUE

The colour of the sky and the sea, blue is traditionally considered to be calming. But richer shades project confidence. They are ideal for contemporary utilitarian schemes and also a striking way to offset heritage industrial features and materials like reclaimed timber.

1 **CHOOSE AN INDUSTRIAL STEEL-BLUE**
(Facing page) Architects Paper House Project completed this home in a former garment factory in east London. The blue-grey walls complement steel-framed interior windows, the shade altering subtly throughout the day with the changing light from the internal atrium. (Left and below) Bespoke joinery firm Christopher Reeve chose a steel-inspired grey-blue for the handcrafted kitchen and home office cabinetry in this Victorian warehouse conversion.

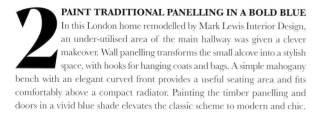

2 **PAINT TRADITIONAL PANELLING IN A BOLD BLUE**
In this London home remodelled by Mark Lewis Interior Design, an under-utilised area of the main hallway was given a clever makeover. Wall panelling transforms the small alcove into a stylish space, with hooks for hanging coats and bags. A simple mahogany bench with an elegant curved front provides a useful seating area and fits comfortably above a compact radiator. Painting the timber panelling and doors in a vivid blue shade elevates the classic scheme to modern and chic.

3 **MATCH VIBRANT UPHOLSTERY TO WALL PANELS**
An eye-catching headboard was a fitting choice for this modern home in a converted upholstery factory in London. While the living area is characterised by raw architectural features, such as exposed brickwork and reclaimed wooden flooring, the master bedroom has a richer and cosier ambience. Mark Lewis Interior Design matched the ridged cobalt blue headboard to the tongue-and-groove wall panelling. The headboard provides a textural contrast to the painted timber.

1.

Ovolo 1888 Darling Harbour

A CONVERTED WOOL STORE WITH COLOURFUL AND CHARACTERFUL INTERIORS

This distinctive hotel is conveniently located in the heart of Sydney, in the Pyrmont district. The area has a rich industrial history, but today the neighbourhood has a tranquil village-like atmosphere. It offers easy access to Darling Harbour, The Rocks and Sydney Fish Market, and the iconic Harbour Bridge is just three kilometres away. Ovolo 1888 is housed in a converted wool store and takes its name from the year in which the old warehouse was built. But the traditional brick and stone façade belies the trendy design-led boutique hotel now housed inside. Here, the old and new are championed. High ceilings and period windows have been retained and original brick exposed. Reclaimed ironbark beams and pillars feature prominently and the guest room desks were crafted from salvaged floorboards. However, there are quirky contemporary twists throughout the hotel too. The award-winning local architecture and interior design firm Luchetti Krelle, engaged on the lobby, public spaces and guest rooms, worked closely with top Australian artists to put the Ovolo stamp on the historic building with vibrant artworks. In the 90 guest rooms, the muted backdrops of bare stone and brick contrast with punchy modern décor, characterised by upholstery in primary colours, Pop Art inspired wall art and black joinery. It is clear that Ovolo 1888 Darling Harbour was conceived with creatives and the young at heart in mind. And its picture-perfect bold and graphic interiors suit the globetrotting Instagram generation. The Ovolo group has achieved a triumphant restoration of one of the oldest of just 21 surviving wool stores in Sydney. But the real success is the way in which this hotel marries historic architecture and up-to-the-minute design and infuses spaces with Australian and Sydney-specific flavour.

3.

1. There is a marked contrast between the exterior of the nineteenth-century wool store and the hotel now inside, which is nothing if not contemporary. Beyond the beautiful stone façade, original features are complemented by chic new décor and Pop Art.

2. The hotel offers two top-notch suites. Split-level suite Shaken has a separate entrance, beneath an enormous stone portico, once used for carriages. Guests here have a private cocktail bar, bathroom with soaking tub and intimate outdoor courtyard.

3. Adaptations of the Sydney-based artist Jasper Knight's works are used as wallpaper and for floor coverings throughout the hotel suites. The vibrant splashes of red, yellow and blue are striking against old brick and are picked up in soft furnishings too.

4. Industrial accents in this Shoebox room include the pegboard clad walls and suspended bare bulb lighting, which reflects shipyard pulleys. The black panelled headboard fits the heritage building but also looks smart and modern alongside the wall art.

REAL HOME

PRIMARY COLOURS

The three primary colours, red, yellow and blue, are mixed to create all the other colours. They are found less frequently in interior design than their innumerable derivatives, but are striking when used in blocks or splashes, especially against expanses of black or white.

CREATE A MODERN SPACE WITH RED, YELLOW AND BLUE
This loft in Tribeca, New York, is located in an Art Deco former industrial building and boasts unobstructed views of Manhattan on three sides. Local architecture practice SheltonMindel designed a continuous unit that wraps around the north, east and west walls of the apartment. It contains heating, ventilation, storage and lighting, but it also serves as an easel for selected artworks. Against the backdrop of white walls and light timber, furniture in primary colours is positioned like abstract forms populating a landscape. Rugs, which mimic the ceiling planes and define different living areas, have narrow yellow bands along their shorter edges. This subtle detailing ties together the primary colour concept, but it also emphasises the width of the space, drawing the eye to the window wall and the remarkable urban vistas.

Whitworth Locke

A TRIO OF COTTON MILLS GIVEN TWENTY FIRST CENTURY TWISTS

Located in the civic quarter of Manchester, in the north of England, Whitworth Locke occupies three connected nineteenth-century buildings. The former cotton mills and textile warehouses required complete renovation. Commissioned to transform the historic structures into a hotel, the American practice Grzywinski + Pons found resonances from some of the firm's earliest work, when it had conceived the interventions to some of New York's nineteenth-century masonry constructions. They drew inspiration from Manchester's industrial heritage too. During the Victorian period, the city led the global finished cotton trade and earned itself the moniker 'Cottonopolis'. Developing the interiors scheme for Whitworth Locke apartment hotel, Grzywinski + Pons selected a palette of colours from the old industrial posters of the 1800s. And, while some of the brick walls have been left in their found state or covered with vibrant wallpaper, many surfaces have been painted various shades of grey in a nod to Manchester's typically overcast skies. The characterful communal areas, which all make the most of the buildings' original features, include a co-working space, bar and café on the ground floor. Every studio apartment is slightly different in its layout and design. Each was conceived as a welcoming home-from-home, with a smart black kitchen, colourful contemporary décor and metal-framed furniture that complements large factory windows. Throughout Whitworth Locke, there are successful juxtapositions of Victorian and modern, raw and refined, tied together by a bold colour scheme that feels at once maverick and modern yet also timeless. The period features and up-to-the-minute decorative touches, as well as the hotel's great amenities, attract design-savvy locals and travellers to visit and linger.

1. The New York studio of Grzywinski + Pons is located on Broadway, in the heart of Manhattan's Cast Iron Historic District. So, as the team started work on Whitworth Locke, they found that many of the historic buildings' proportions, materials and textures were familiar. They felt a strong sense of responsibility to preserve and promote old features.

2. A glass atrium linking the buildings, but used as a service road, was entirely renovated and now houses The Conservatory bar. Potted plants hang from its apex and are dotted throughout its seating areas, matched by a foliage printed wallpaper. The apricot-coloured Silo lighting by Zero makes subtle reference to a classic industrial form above the bar.

3. In the hotel's 160 spacious guest rooms, the walls are painted salmon pink and are offset by the pistachio green upholstery. This uplifting colour palette was inspired by vintage posters advertising trade links between Manchester and "warmer and brighter corners of the globe". The distinctive mix gives a light, modern twist to an industrial aesthetic.

4. Most of the furniture and all of the joinery was designed by Grzywinski + Pons. Slatted timber headboards complement reeded glass industrial-inspired wardrobes. Understated lighting designs suit the painted brick walls and exposed piping to further enhance the cool utilitarian aesthetic in Whitworth Locke's one-of-a-kind guest apartments.

4.

PASTELS

There is a lighter side to industrial styling, which can be achieved through the use
of delicate pastels. Introduce gentle tints through painted joinery as well as smaller items
of furniture, lighting and decorative accessories for a 'barely there' approach to colour.

CREATE BRIGHT MODERN SPACES WITH SUBTLE COLOURS

Taiwanese studio HAO Design completed Starburst House in Beijing for a young couple with a small child. The interior designers took advantage of the property's asymmetric pitched roof and inserted a mezzanine to create a more spacious family home filled with natural light. Thick-set concrete steps lead to the newly created upper level, which houses a gallery library and small work area. On the ground floor there is an open-plan living area, furnished with a grey sofa, and dining area dressed with soft pink, blue and light wood dining chairs and a pale green factory-style pendant lamp. Light hues have also been applied in the kitchen, which has pale blue cabinetry and a glossy white subway tile splashback. Sliding room dividers facilitate partitioning and create privacy when required. The building's gable roof is emphasised by a feature wall of white brick slip, appropriate for a softened industrial look. Practical pegboard surfaces also suit the subtle utilitarian influences. But it is HAO Design's use of a light material palette and muted pastel colours that completes this bright and airy contemporary family loft.

2.

The Silo

A ONE-OF-A-KIND HOTEL IN AN ICONIC GRAIN SILO

The grain silo towering over the V&A Waterfront in Cape Town was decommissioned in 2001 after nearly 80 years at the heart of South Africa's agricultural industry. At 187 feet, it was once the tallest building in Sub-Saharan Africa. Today, following a bold transformation, the base of the former silo houses the Zeitz Museum of Contemporary Art Africa, while the grain elevator has been converted into The Silo Hotel over six floors. Liz Biden, co-owner of The Royal Portfolio hotels, had a singular vision for a new offering that would capture the essence of her home city, Cape Town. The exterior of the hotel was designed by the award-winning British design and architecture practice Heatherwick Studio. The most significant intervention to the original structure was the insertion of 18-foot high windows into the hotel floors. These bulbous multi-faceted additions display the influence of classic factory windows in their geometry, but were also directly inspired by grain kernels. And in many ways, the scale of these windows influenced the hotel's décor. The views of Table Mountain and Table Bay harbour have to be seen to be believed. But Liz Biden has created inimitable interior experiences as well. Egyptian chandeliers hang over Persian rugs, European and Asian antiques appear alongside African art, while jewel-coloured silks, velvets and leather offset industrial materials. This bold approach extends to the 28 guest rooms (including a one-bedroom penthouse), each of which were individually designed. A grain silo originally constructed in 1921 might not have seemed an obvious choice for a stylish new hotel, but this concrete monolith in the heart of South Africa's Mother City has been reborn as a travel destination in itself. For a boutique family-owned hotel, The Silo certainly packs a punch.

3.

"We created interiors to complement the stark industrial architecture, balancing raw features with stylish, comfortable decorative elements."

LIZ BIDEN, THE ROYAL PORTFOLIO

1. In The Silo Hotel's lobby, bare concrete walls are decorated with colourful and eclectic artworks by emerging as well as established African artists. The sculptural chandelier by Haldane Martin is a striking feature juxtaposed with old grain hoppers.

2. The redeveloped grain silo successfully contrasts historic infrastructure with vivid modern designs and local references. Preserved machinery at the hotel entrance, and throughout the conversion, honours the building's past and appears sculptural.

3. The hotel's furnishings inject bold hits of colour against industrial features. In The Willaston Bar, blue button-studded velvet and leather upholstery offsets black structural steels. Circular chandeliers mimic the steel rings once used in the grain elevator.

REAL HOME

REAL HOME

VIBRANT COLOURS

From bright artworks and upholstery in statement hues to structural features painted
in daring shades, there are a number of ways to complete a bold industrial-inspired scheme.
Brave and brilliant homeowners are embracing every opportunity to use vibrant colours.

INFUSE INTERIORS WITH ENERGY AND VIVID CHARACTER

Commissioned to transform the London home of artist and designer Cleo Barbour, Alexander Owen Architecture drew creative inspiration from her colourful projects. Working in close collaboration with their client, who was excited to push boundaries with colours, fabrics and fixtures, the studio adopted a more curatorial role, enabling Cleo to deliver her unique style architecturally. The apartment is a riot of colour and yet its appearance is cool and considered. The largest wall runs double height and forms one side of the open-plan living area, dining space and mezzanine bedroom. It was given an ombre treatment in tropical turquoise that is reminiscent of cocktails and tie dye. Turquoise was also selected to highlight steel beams, kitchen cabinets and the spiral staircase that leads to the bedroom. Flashes of bright pink were introduced through artworks, while a large sofa was upholstered in lilac. To complete the look, trusses were painted bright pink, as was an old scaffold board fashioned into a long under-window bookshelf.

1.

Soho Warehouse

A FORMER FACTORY AND ONE TIME RECORDING STUDIO

The members' club and hotel Soho Warehouse is located, as its name suggests, in a converted warehouse building in downtown Los Angeles. Originally constructed in 1916, it later housed a recording studio in the 1970s. As with all Soho House outposts, during the two-year transformation of the former warehouse, the group's design team focused on honouring the property's past and the surrounding area's distinctive culture. Exposed brick walls, ceiling pipework and pillars immediately create an industrial aesthetic, this grittiness enhanced by 1970s graffiti which was left on bare surfaces. The graffiti tags bring colour and graphic forms to the public spaces and reference the neighbourhood's street art. Art Deco elements reflect when the building was constructed, but are also a nod to Soho Warehouse's location in Los Angeles' arts district. Homage is further paid to the local community through many commissioned artworks on display throughout the members' club and hotel, including an acrylic-on-canvas by Paul Davies and a mural by Blanda. Other collaborations include customised, locally-made furniture, art and textiles. There are 1970s style jewel-toned velvet sofas and shaggy rugs. This site-specific approach is a distinctive blueprint of Soho House and it is exemplified in the way these eclectic design elements are expertly brought together. This extends to the 48 spacious loft-like bedrooms, which feature vintage pieces alongside custom-made furniture items. Larger bedrooms, designed for longer stays, are each equipped with a kitchenette and dining table, a walk-in wardrobe and freestanding bathtub. Soho House is a revolutionary brand catering to a trendy crowd of creatives and industry insiders. Whether visiting for work or leisure, visitors will find that Soho Warehouse hums with energy.

1. Soho Warehouse guest bedrooms were designed to resemble artists' lofts. The Large category rooms offer a kitchenette, dining area and L-shaped sofa, inviting relaxation. In this room, a sliding industrial door behind the kingsize bed leads to the bathroom.

2. Artworks curated in collaboration with local downtown galleries can be seen on every floor of the property. An original loading dock door beside the entrance is adorned with a bright, specially commissioned mural by street artist Shepard Fairey.

3. A neutral palette ensures the bare brickwork and preserved graffiti tags remain the focus in the Drawing Room. But graphic prints selected for some of the upholstery bring additional colour to the funky furniture shapes and suit the edgy wall art.

4. The Soho House team scoured local LA design and vintage stores, including Dex Vintage, Simon St. James and Lawson Fenning to achieve Soho Warehouse's one-off interiors. The eclectic spaces cater perfectly for creatives working and relaxing.

GET THE LOOK

GET THE LOOK

STREET ART

Since the 1960s, graffiti has relayed the grit and energy of the urban environment. More recently, it has moved indoors and is now bringing unexpected edginess to interiors. Tags, throw-ups, drips and splatters introduce pattern, colour and city culture to interior design.

1 GIVE ANY WALL A COLOURFUL GRUNGY MAKEOVER

The Urban Art On Metal wallpaper mural by Hovia (left) is a replica of a genuine graffiti artwork. It is a bestseller for those who are fond of street artistry and want to channel the look at home. The wallpaper not only recreates the paint colours, it also mimics the corrugated metal onto which they were originally sprayed. Similarly, the Street Art mural by Rebel Walls (above) brings urban character to any space, depicting graffiti on a white brick wall. It will transform any room or hallway.

2 OPT FOR ADVENTUROUS UPHOLSTERY FABRICS

Graffiti Stripe Velvet by Timorous Beasties is a maelstrom of paint drips, aerosol motifs and ink wash. As disobedient and daring as street art itself, this contemporary fabric contrasts effectively with the clean and classic lines of the Noelle Sofa by British design studio Pinch. The sofa's slim high scroll arms form a timeless silhouette. The straight back and sides and deep cushion offer plenty of flat surfaces, giving the impression the paint was applied directly to the furniture.

4 INSERT HUMOROUS AND QUIRKY TOUCHES

Classical art meets modern-day street art in the irreverent Monsieur Mint velvet cushion, created by the anglo-Italian design duo Young & Battaglia for their own interiors brand Mineheart. The appropriately named Funky Undercover Antique Plates, also by Young & Battaglia, bring graffiti art to classic pure white porcelain. Traditional and quaint scenes of country life have been given a contemporary twist in vibrant splashes to suit any home and table.

3 TRANSFORM ANY FLOOR WITH A GRAFFITI RUG

Jan Kath is one of the world's most well-known rug designers. Graffity is included in Kath's Unknown Artists collection. The German creative transposed the street artworks by anonymous sprayers from the cities of Los Angeles and New York to create a range of original wool and silk floor coverings. More than 150,000 knots per square metre are used to bring the shades and scripts to life and transfer underground artworks to a new format that can be appreciated under foot.

Stamba Hotel

A SOVIET ERA PUBLISHING HOUSE FULL OF INDUSTRIAL CHARACTER

Located within Vera, a characterful historic quarter of Tbilisi, is a design hotel that uniquely encapsulates the vibrant and creative ambience of the Georgian capital. Stamba Hotel is located within the former headquarters of a Soviet printing house, and Adjara Group Holding's in-house team of architects and interior designers clearly placed great emphasis on preserving as much as possible of its original character. A lot of the old printing machinery was retained in the public spaces, including the print-drying beam in the atrium, while Soviet-era lights hang in the café. In transforming the previously abandoned brutalist structure, care was also taken to create a design-led hotel that reflected the zeitgeist of modern-day Tbilisi, a city often referred to as 'the Caucasian Paris'. The hotel's up-to-the-minute amenities include an amphitheatre for live music and theatre performances and a photography museum. In addition, there is a music library from which guests can loan vinyls to play on their in-room stereos. In fact, the 62 bedrooms invite guests to relax and unwind. They are notably spacious, with high ceilings and rough industrial characteristics. Bookcases are well stocked with vacation reading and works by Georgian artists add lively local touches to the accommodation's welcoming atmosphere. The sage-painted feature walls are a striking contrast to the rooms' bare concrete and orange-brown exposed brickwork. The green shade adds warmth while also referencing the abundant plant life in the hotel lobby and courtyard gardens. Wedged between Europe and Asia, Tbilisi attracts tourists with its distinctive cultural blend and historic sights. Stamba Hotel also bridges old and new, offering its visitors a unique insight into Georgia's past and future, and a different take on industrial interiors.

3.

1. Four floors were removed in the hotel's lobby to create a soaring space, which has been fitted with expansive metal bookshelving. Portions of the old concrete structures and brickwork are painted steel blue, drawing further attention to the fabric of the twentieth-century brutalist landmark building and underscoring the lobby's industrial chic aesthetic.

2. The large warehouse windows reinforce the raw industrial character of the former printing house and blur the boundary between Stamba Hotel's interior spaces and the outside world. Trees and vines, planted throughout the public spaces, also serve to invite the outdoors in, while softening the forms and textures of industrial materials on display.

3. The uncovered concrete ceilings of the rooms have been painted white. The treatment maximises the natural light and sense of space, while exposed metal conduit and simple lighting reinforce a cool industrial aesthetic. Floor-to-ceiling bookshelves in this suite draw further attention to the ceiling height but also generate a more homely atmosphere.

4. In this Aviator room, full-height double doors slide back to reveal the bathroom. Meanwhile, each of the Signature Aviator rooms (3) channel open-plan loft living, with freestanding polished brass bathtubs set immediately beside the bedroom and blurring the distinction between spaces. Brass fittings in all guest bathrooms add a touch of luxury.

GET THE LOOK

COLOURED CONCRETE

If raw concrete is considered too stark for a scheme, there are a wealth of designs, large and small, that incorporate colour. These furniture, homeware and lighting creations combine the textural qualities of heavy-duty concrete with soft shades to suit any home.

1 BRING COLOURED CONCRETE TO THE BATHROOM
This sophisticated soft industrial bathroom scheme was conceived by Elisabetta Bongiorni of Terzo Piano for Fiandre Architectural Surfaces. It features Fiandre's Fjord collection concrete-effect tiles as well as a pair of blush pink surface-mounted concrete basins by specialist British firm Kast. The Rho basin, shown, is one of a wide variety of designs by Kast, which range from simple to contoured and patterned options. High-quality pigments are blended for a palette of 28 lovely colours.

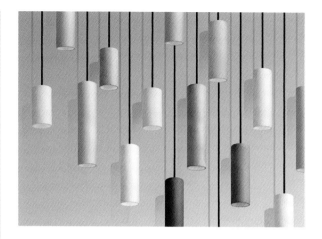

3 HANG UNCONVENTIONAL CONCRETE DESIGNS
This collection of elegant modern concrete pendant lights is handmade in a workshop in Rome, Italy, and available from Dyke & Dean. The minimalist lights, formed from ultra-thin concrete, are available in three different sizes and 12 different colours, including burgundy, sage green, yellow and blue. Each lamp gives focused light for the surface below. Mixing and matching colours and sizes creates a dynamic lighting installation in residential and commercial settings.

2 SELECT STYLISH SEATING WITH A DIFFERENCE
Fade Drum by Brooklyn-based artist Fernando Mastrangelo is cast entirely from hand-dyed cement, with a hollow cavity in the centre. The stool is made to order and poured into a fibreglass mould in individual layers, from top to bottom. Finally, the piece is carefully sanded to a polished finish and then sealed. Fade Drum's subtle ombre effect in pastel shades is reminiscent of watercolour paintings, imbuing a stool formed from industrial cement with an unexpected softness.

4 GROUP TOGETHER CONCRETE ACCESSORIES
The Chimney Containers by Marta Bakowski are a family of vessels handcrafted in tinted cement. The artist, who lives in Paris, often explores and celebrates colour and material in her creative output. The Chimney Containers demonstrate the potential to make attractive homeware and sculptural pieces using a commonplace construction material. Assembling each vessel using different coloured and shaped components reinforces a successful play on opposites.

Feature Furnishings

Hero items of furniture or décor are like leading characters in a play, taking centre stage in the production and interacting in a particularly noteworthy or memorable way with the wider setting and the rest of the cast. In industrial-style interiors, the key furnishings might be chosen to directly reference or counterbalance any older original features. Designs might be vintage or contemporary, classic or quirky, but scale, material and colour all play a crucial role in their selection and suitability. There are budget-friendly choices and investment pieces, and these can be successfully juxtaposed within a space. From wall and floor coverings to wow-factor large-scale furniture and one-off decorative touches, there are a number of clever ways to ensure any room scheme steals the show.

The dramatic upholstered headboards at Ovolo Woolloomooloo, Sydney, were specially commissioned for the hotel and were a creative collaboration by Australian hospitality furnishings specialist firms Materialised and Cairncross Martin. The custom-made panelled designs feature an array of colourful graphics printed onto a waterproof base linen. The wrap-around form frames the sleeping area and adds drama to the bedroom.

Hotel Emma

A CONVERTED BREWERY WITH AN AUTHENTIC SPIRIT

Set on the riverfront, Hotel Emma is housed in a nineteenth century brewery in the historic Pearl district on the northern edge of downtown San Antonio, Texas. The hotel is a majestic focal point for the neighbourhood and a lasting reminder of the area's craft heritage. New York-based design studio Roman and Williams, entrusted with the transformation of the former Pearl Brewery, is renowned for the way in which many of its completed projects show a successful interplay between old and new. And the practice's thoughtful treatment of this San Antonio landmark has resulted in the sense that Hotel Emma is in fact a brewery lying dormant, ready to spring back to life at any moment. The interiors combine South Texas charm with preserved industrial character, a timeless elegance with large heavy-duty machinery and raw architectural features. Today, the cellars are used for receptions and events, while the cavernous former brewing halls offer excellent dining and spaces to unwind with a craft brew or book from the impressive two-storey library. Exposed brickwork and peeling plaster are juxtaposed with hand-tooled leather and buffalo hides. Heavy-duty equipment, cast-iron tanks and towering architecture stand over intimate, inviting social spaces. Fermentation tanks now contain inviting banquette seating. Old beer-bottling equipment has been imaginatively repurposed as light fixtures. Meanwhile, the distinctive and spacious guest rooms offer high ceilings and low lighting, utilitarian textures and warm furnishings. Originally built in 1894, and named after Pearl Brewery's heroic Prohibition-era owner, Hotel Emma has a rich and colourful backstory. But this remarkable industrial conversion, at once unconventional and full of character, will be writing compelling new chapters for years to come.

1. The rich textures of the lobby, with its exposed brick and concrete walls, set the tone for visitors' experience of Hotel Emma. Enormous industrial fixtures, such as the fly wheel of an old generator, are offset by the bespoke oversized brass, bronze and blown-glass chandeliers punctuating the space.

2. The patterned encaustic concrete tiles laid in the lobby sensitively replicate the former brewery's original flooring. The tiles pick out colours in the vintage kilim rugs also adorning the floors. Leather button-backed armchairs and Moroccan ottomans invite guests to stay and savour the unique ambience.

3. In the Sternewirth Bar and Clubroom, set in the great hall with its soaring 25-feet-high ceilings, huge cast-iron tanks and concrete pillars soar over intimate seating areas. The lower-level steampunk-inspired studded leather seating further emphasises the dramatic proportions of the preserved structures.

4. The guest bathroom walls feature tiles in cream and watery blue, custom-designed by Roman and Williams. The glazed tiles have a rustic finish that suits the heritage building. Elegant white porcelain vanities, brass faucets and 1900s-inspired lighting also underscore the subtle charm of the bathrooms.

5. Each of the 146 guest bedrooms has its own unique personality. Rooms located in the original Brewhouse tower are particularly noteworthy. Raw industrial features, including exposed plaster and brick detailing, combine with classic luxury décor, such as the beautifully crisp white Frette bed linen.

6. The tones and patterns of the bare plaster walls create so much visual interest and character that the rest of the décor can be relatively understated. Humble handcrafted wooden furniture with saddle hide leather is juxtaposed with traditional iron-framed beds and soft furnishings with simple prints.

TILES

Durable and easy to maintain, tiles are an ideal decorative choice for modern homes and particularly well-suited to kitchens and bathrooms. Used en masse, they are also an effective way to introduce alternative textures, as well as colour and pattern, into a scheme.

LAYING TILES DIFFERENTIATES BETWEEN FUNCTIONAL SPACES AND CREATES A FEATURE IN AN OPEN-PLAN HOME

The De Havilland building in Hackney, London, was designed in the 1930s by Sir Owen Williams, one of Britain's foremost architects of the period. Originally used for the manufacturing of aviation parts, the former factory was converted for residential use in 1998. Feix & Merlin Architects were commissioned by the owner of this apartment to realise its full potential from an empty shell. The practice designed a new mezzanine structure, with a bedroom above and a study and large bathroom below. Reclaimed windows and doors and coloured glass panels were inserted into the wall between the open-plan kitchen and bathroom, achieving visual interest. Saffron yellow tiles were sourced by the client for the bathroom. Blue tiles on the back wall and floor of the eat-in kitchen contrast strikingly with the concrete ceiling and create a demarcation between kitchen and living areas.

Wm. Mulherin's Sons

A CONVERTED WHISKEY FACTORY IN PHILADELPHIA'S COOL FISHTOWN QUARTER

This boutique hotel is named after the Irish family that operated a whiskey blending and bottling factory here in the late nineteenth century. The landmarked three-floor red brick building, originally constructed in 1890, was restored by Method Co, a Philadelphia-based developer and operator of independent hospitality projects. Method retained many of its period features, including large arched windows and timber flooring. Exposed ductwork and pipes enhance the industrial character of the property. But there are some more unusual relics from the old factory's past too. Lift shafts have been converted into skylights, barrel-weighing scales and pulley systems remain in place. And in one guest room, an original vault now contains an inviting claw-footed bath tub. There are just four rooms at Wm. Mulherin's Sons. Each is essentially a spacious studio, featuring a fully-equipped kitchen and enabling guests to live as locals do. The interiors are charming, combining bare brick walls and timber panelling with an understated colour palette, a quirky specially-designed wallpaper, leather seating and vintage rugs. There are custom-made items of wooden furniture by Tim Lewis Studio, such as the beautiful bed headboards, and industrial-inspired lighting from Roll & Hill and Workstead. Plants and cacti add to the home-from-home ambience. The superb ground-floor Italian restaurant, which opened before the rooms and is now a key reason to stay at Wm. Mulherin's Sons, is widely regarded as one of the finest eateries in Philadelphia. It offers an 'urban rustic' wood-fire menu, which is enjoyed at fireside tables and in cosy dining booths. All in all, Wm. Mulherin's Sons seems to be setting the bar for boutique hospitality in Philadelphia, its restaurant and rooms impressing locals and out-of-towners alike.

1. The restaurant and bar at Wm. Mulherin's Sons serves wood-fired Italian fare in a wood-panelled setting with industrial touches and cosy fireside area.

2. Wm. Mulherin's Sons is located in the trendy Fishtown neighbourhood of Philadelphia, which is known for its restaurants, galleries and music venues.

3. Room Three still has the building's original lift shaft, repurposed as a new skylight. The preserved hardwood floor is complemented by vintage rugs.

4. Every room has a well-equipped kitchen with walnut frameless cabinets, concrete counters and glazed tiles inspired by whiskey bottles found on site.

5. Wallpaper designer Evan Raney and illustrator Stacy Rozich created a bespoke toile for the hotel that is a quirky contrast to the rooms' old features.

GET THE LOOK

RUGS

Available in an incredible array of sizes, shades and styles, rugs immediately transform rooms. They soften the effect of industrial features, by introducing colour, pattern and texture, and anchor furniture while defining separate functional areas in open-plan spaces.

1 EMBRACE A VINTAGE EFFECT
The Erased Heritage collection by rug designer Jan Kath pays homage to a variety of traditional Oriental carpet styles, from Egyptian Mamluks and Iranian Bidjars to Turkish Konyas. Kath drew inspiration from old patterns and techniques and worked with master weavers to bring new life to classic designs. A unique finishing method has given a modern twist to the carpets, while also creating the impression that they have lain on floors for years, becoming worn or distressed.

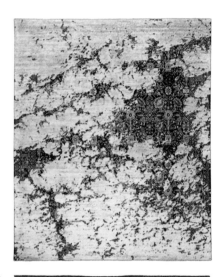

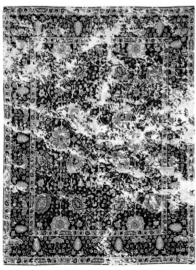

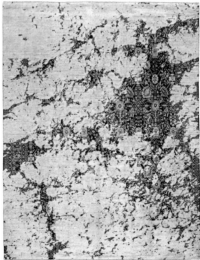

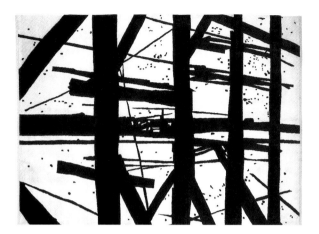

3 CHOOSE A DESIGN THAT ECHOES OLD FEATURES

For over 30 years, Christopher Farr has produced modern rugs in collaboration with established artists and designers. This handknotted rug of handspun wool brings to life a piece by British artist Tony Bevan, who is known for his graphic style with distressed line work and distorted geometries. Rafters depicts the criss-crossing timbers found in roof construction. It is ideally suited to heritage warehouse conversions but will also inject industrial style into new homes.

2 RECREATE INDUSTRIAL SHADES AND PATTERNS

London-based rug supplier Floor Story is known for its wide-ranging collection and its collaborative capsule projects with leading and emerging designers. Ibis (top left), Transition (top right) and Textura (above) are particularly noteworthy for any industrial-inspired scheme. Each of these hand-knotted wool and silk rugs recreates raw surfaces. Textura, by Venezuelan designer Adriana Jaroslavsky, was inspired by peeling pink paint on an old weather-worn green water tank.

4 CHANNEL THE LATEST TRENDS IN A NEW WAY

Portuguese brand Rug'Society aims to transform rugs into captivating works of art and is continually influenced by emerging interiors and fashion trends. For those choosing not to invest in terrazzo flooring itself, this Terrazzo rug is a cost-effective and attractive way to channel the look of the hard composite material while also retaining softer textures in a space. The light tones and scattered design make the rug an appealing choice for any room of the home.

Wythe Hotel

A HISTORIC BROOKLYN FACTORY TURNED BOUTIQUE HOTEL

The first luxury offering in Williamsburg when it opened in 2012, Wythe Hotel remains one of the most desirable places to stay in this hip New York City neighbourhood. Located on the Williamsburg waterfront, in Brooklyn, Wythe Hotel has uninterrupted views of the Manhattan skyline. The building started life in 1901 as a barrel-making factory and was redeveloped by Two Trees Management, who pioneered much of the rehabilitation of Brooklyn's old industrial DUMBO district. New York firm Morris Adjmi Architects was commissioned to rework the brick, cast-iron and timber-frame factory building and inserted one all-glass façade, which gives all of the west-facing rooms panoramic Manhattan views through warehouse-style windows. A contemporary four-storey glazed rooftop extension was also added to the former cooperage. Internally, many of the building's heritage features were carefully preserved. There are concrete floors, arched windows and cast-iron support columns. Reynard, the restaurant at the Wythe, has a beautiful tiled floor, floor-to-ceiling vintage glass doors and substantial industrial-style chandeliers. The 70 bedrooms all boast 13-feet-high original timber ceilings and sizeable windows and are filled with natural light. Some have exposed brickwork. The surplus ceiling pine was also cleverly repurposed to construct bed frames and desks. The guest rooms have heated concrete floors and are minimally decorated, allowing the building's character and city views to do the talking. Wythe Hotel is often cited as an exemplar of sensitive restoration, with interiors that are respectful of the former factory's heritage yet also distinctive and modern with contributions from local creatives. In many ways, this echoes the transformation of Williamsburg, from industrial district to flourishing design quarter.

1. The Brooklyn-based design studio Workstead was responsible for the public spaces. In the lobby, the metal overhead rail formerly used to transport materials around the cooperage was left in situ. It is juxtaposed with industrial chic bare bulb lighting.

2. The hotel library, located off the lobby, features custom-built glazed display bookcases which offset the exposed brickwork of the heritage building. Mid-century-style armchairs and black bentwood chairs enable guests to stay and enjoy their reading.

3. The New York-based artist Dan Funderburgh designed three custom wallpapers for Wythe Hotel, produced by Flavor Paper. Cooperage is a tribute to the specialist tools and craftsmanship historically involved in barrel-making in delicate blue and white.

4. Prior to the old factory's careful restoration, its timber ceilings were in disrepair and its brick walls were damaged as well as defaced with graffiti. Now, the traces of the building's history still evident are a visual link between the hotel's interiors and locality.

GET THE LOOK

SCENERY WALLPAPER

"Whatever you have in your rooms," advised William Morris, "think first of the walls; for they are that which makes your house and home." Today, wallpapers which put a modern twist on classic toiles, etchings and industrial vignettes are a quirky way to transform a space.

1 COMMISSION A LOCALLY-INSPIRED PRINT DESIGN

Wythe Toile (left) and Cooperage (right) were designed for Wythe Hotel, Williamsburg, by local illustrator Dan Funderburgh and were printed by bespoke wallpaper specialists Flavor Paper. After thoroughly researching the building's past, the artist created three custom designs based on its time serving as a cooperage, rope-making plant and eventually as a warehouse used by skaters and BMX riders. The papers have different styles but were all printed in the same steel blue colourway.

2 CONSIDER CORK AS AN ALTERNATIVE TO PAPER

Hit The North is an original alternative to wallpaper, produced by The Monkey Puzzle Tree and available from Dowsing & Reynolds. It features an intricate graphic design by artist Drew Millward, depicting the industrial architecture of the north of England printed onto sustainable Portuguese cork. While Millward is best known for creating psychedelic posters for rock bands like Foo Fighters, this Modernist-inspired textured cork wallcovering has a rock'n'roll quality too.

3 CHOOSE A COLOURFUL PATTERN FOR CHILDREN

Factory Town is a playful wallpaper, created by Los Angeles-based illustrator and creative director Stephanie Birdsong and available from Spoonflower. The whimsical design in pinks and greys shows miniature factories and smoke stacks amid trees and winding rivers. The pattern and colours make the paper a charming choice for a child's room. As it is a water-activated removable wallpaper, it is a simple solution for renters and an effortless way to create a feature wall.

4 SELECT A PAPER WITH A HANDSKETCHED LOOK

'Taxi Jeune' was hand-designed by Sandrine Coureau for the luxury French fabric and wallpaper company Pierre Frey. It is a large-scale illustration of New York, which shows the city's iconic rooftop water towers and the architecture of Greenwich Village and Brooklyn. The painterly quality of the paper, which is available in a colourful pastel version as well as grey tones, makes it an ideal choice for heritage and modern homes and for anyone with a love of the Big Apple.

5 CHANNEL THE EDGIER ASPECTS OF CITY LIVING

London Toile, by Scottish designers Timorous Beasties, might initially call to mind the traditional French *toile de jouy* wallpaper of the 1800s. But upon closer inspection, the print displays an irreverence and dark humour, combining vignettes of iconic London architecture such as St Paul's Cathedral and Tower Bridge with gritty scenes of urban life, including a mugging. The wallpaper is available in three colourways and can also be combined with the London Toile linen.

The Collective Paper Factory

A RADIO FACTORY TURNED PAPER MILL IN NEW YORK THAT IS NOW A COOL HOTEL

This factory, constructed in 1922, was first used by the Pilot Radio Company for the construction of radios and radio parts. During World War Two, the plant went into the production of communication devices. As paper production began to soar, due to the newspaper industry boom during the war, the site then became a paper mill. By 1970, however, the building and neighbourhood had fallen into neglect. The area experienced a resurgence during the 'dot com' era, but it wasn't until 2012 that a developer saw potential in the industrial complex at its heart. Today, The Paper Factory hotel is owned by The Collective, a group which creates modern co-working and co-living destinations, and welcomes guests from one to 29 nights. It retains or reclaims many original features, with polished concrete floors, exposed piping and vintage hammered metal doors. 12-feet-high ceilings and expansive windows fill the public spaces and guest rooms with light. Mixed metals combine with a range of upcycled elements and vibrant artworks. The spacious guest rooms have all been well designed. Industrial-inspired metal and reclaimed timber furniture complements warm brickwork and original columns. The Manhattan loft rooms feature separate living areas and kitchenettes, encouraging a slower pace of life in a design-led setting. The sun-drenched conservatory and courtyard are other inviting places for guests to kick-back. The Collective Paper Factory stands at the heart of Queens, a symbol of the district's industrial past and more recent regeneration and a hotel that draws on local culture. With a range of workspaces and lounges, this former factory where labourers once toiled through lengthy shifts now offers plenty of comfortable and creative environments for those who need to work during their visit.

1. While The Collective Paper Factory's interiors are modern and inviting, there are several tributes throughout the hotel to a pre-digital age, from the restored original features to reclaimed industrial furniture. In the conservatory, factory pallet tables mix with antique-style seating for an eclectic look.

2. The Collective design team enlisted the input of Palette Architecture for the hotel's new renovation. This included a range of public spaces, designed to host daily experiences, from music programmes to educational gatherings and business workshops. Several interconnected spaces offer living-room seating arrangements. Colourful artwork and plush furniture contrast with timber wall-cladding and the converted factory's slick polished concrete floors.

3. Standard King guest rooms are among the most popular at the hotel, offering plenty of space to rest and recharge. Modern rustic and industrial-style furniture is softened by the calming colour palette and eye-catching canvas artworks, capturing the historic and more hip characteristics of Queens itself.

BOOKS

From dusty old paperbacks to modern tomes and colour-coordinated collections, books can be put to imaginative use in interior design. There are innumerable ways to store, stack and display treasured reading material and bookshelving can make a bold statement.

PLAY WITH PERSPECTIVE FOR ADDED VISUAL INTEREST

Publisher's Loft is an open-plan apartment in Williamsburg, New York, that was designed by Büro Koray Duman for a publisher and a furniture dealer. The clients had an extensive collection of over 2,500 books, which posed a challenge for the architects and a property measuring 1,200 square feet. Their ingenious solution was to design a library that wrapped around the property. The shelving serves as a backdrop to the dining room and lines a corridor running from the living room, past the bathroom, and into the bedroom. The custom shelving is set at 45 degrees, meaning books can be viewed from one direction while being disguised behind a series of elegant 'columns' from the other. The white-painted custom-built joinery contrasts effectively with the old industrial building's original timbers and exposed aluminium ductwork. The timber and tile flooring, which was laid on the diagonal, also draws the eye to the clever angled bookshelving design feature.

Ovolo Woolloomooloo

A CONVERTED WATERFRONT WAREHOUSE FULL OF MODERN DESIGN AND COLOUR

In the heart of the city's Central Business District, yet situated on the waterfront in a peaceful wharf, Ovolo Hotel Woolloomooloo offers the very best for a stay in Sydney. Finger Wharf is over a century old, the oldest of its kind in Australia. After a bold transformation, it is now available to visitors and locals to enjoy. Ovolo is an energetic brand and a playful aesthetic reflects this. But careful consideration has also been paid to showcasing the heritage building's remarkable features. Contrasts between old and new are celebrated throughout the hotel and it abounds with characterful designs and artworks. Award-winning architecture practice Hassell had an ingenious solution for the immense atrium. Playhouse-like structures break up the floorplan into smaller zones, providing more intimate spaces within the soaring warehouse conversion. There is an inviting central bar,

work stations, pool table and retro arcade games, encouraging hotel visitors to unwind and have fun. Pastel-coloured kissing booths have pull-down blinds and offer a little seclusion for drinks and nibbles. The 100 spacious, beautifully designed private rooms and loft suites continue the exuberant atmosphere of the hotel's public spaces. The enormous structural steels and warehouse windows set the tone and are complemented by the rooms' joyful colour palettes, with selected eclectic furnishings, striking lighting and modern artworks. Top-tier split-level pad Ultraroo is worthy of a special mention for its private circular cocktail bar. As are the large and bright ensuite bathrooms. Ovolo Hotel Woolloomooloo is just a short stroll from Sydney's most famous sights, such as The Royal Botanic Garden, Harbour Bridge and iconic Sydney Opera House. But heritage-listed Finger Wharf and this cool warehouse hotel should be on everyone's checklist too.

3.

1.& 2. A series of internal pavilions provide more intimate spaces within the cavernous interior of the warehouse conversion. The approach maintains the sense of the heritage building's impressive scale and enables guests to enjoy both the old and the new.

3. The Piper Room is the only part of the wharf that remains in its original condition. Its wooden floorboards and high ceilings imbue it with charm and industrial character. A versatile space, it is very popular for events but worth a peek for hotel guests.

4.& 5. The hotel's design capitalises on light. The skylights in the roof brighten the vast atrium by day. Full-sized trees illuminated with LEDs form a romantic streetscape leading to a central bar, Alibi. Fairground-style lighting is another quirky feature.

6. The 100 guest bedrooms offer plenty to admire, whether it is the remarkable city or waterfront vistas or the vibrant décor. Through a partnership with government initiative Artbank, the rooms are hung with original contemporary Australian works of art.

7. In every room, the bed takes centre stage with a dramatic custom-made oversized headboard that surrounds the head of the bed and bedside units. The headboard creates the sense of being cocooned and is particularly effective when near an entryway.

8. The enormous industrial structures in many of the former warehouse rooms now frame the chic modern furniture. Low-level seating along the full width of the sizeable windows highlights the scale of the features and lets guests savour the outlooks.

GET THE LOOK

FEATURE BEDS

A good bed is an important investment. How we sleep affects how we live. But as one of the largest items in a home, a beautifully designed bed can also have a dramatic effect on an interior scheme. From classic to contemporary, a hero bed is what dreams are made of.

CHOOSE A UNIQUE HEADBOARD FOR BEDROOM DRAMA

Savoir Beds is internationally renowned for exceptionally crafted mattresses and remarkable headboards, handmade using time-honoured techniques and the finest quality upholstery fabrics. The Shift 01 headboard (left) is the result of a collaboration between Savoir Beds and the designer Arik Levy. It has a functional construction, with upholstered panels which can be moved from side to side, adjusting the bed's appearance and creating useful shelves. The B Bed (right) was conceived with Christian Lacroix creative director Sacha Walckhoff and features stacked side modules that serve as bedside units as well as display boxes for books and favourite objects. Its oversized proportions particularly suit conversions with high ceilings. But traditional headboards upholstered in luxurious materials are an impactful choice too.

Dexamenes

A SEASIDE RETREAT WITH DISTINCTIVE INDUSTRIAL FLAIR

This abandoned wine factory is set right on the seafront on Greece's Peloponnese coast. The industrial architecture has been minimally altered to convert the former plant into a contemporary hotel. Greek design firm K-Studio identified a unique opportunity to convert two parallel concrete and steel-framed blocks of wine tanks. The tanks, which measured approximately five metres by six metres, were the perfect size for guest bedrooms, each incorporating an ensuite bathroom and many also offering a canopy-shaded patio. And so today, Dexamenes seaside hotel offers the remarkable experience of sleeping inside 1920s wine tanks. The rich patina of their bare concrete walls sets the tone for the calm and clean-lined interiors, combining frosted glass, black metal frameworks and pale timber. The textured glass panels ensure natural light penetrates each room from the window cut into its concrete exterior. The polished terrazzo floors suit the Greek climate as well as the industrial chic scheme. Black metal pipework echoes aspects of the old factory's construction, framing the bathrooms and open dressing areas and completing the monastic yet modern spaces. The area between the two accommodation blocks is a peaceful water garden, providing a cooling breeze throughout the hotel. Standing in the middle of the shallow pool are two sizeable old steel drums which provide quiet spaces for rest and relaxation. Grapes and currants line the edges of the garden, reflecting the site's history. Visitors can enjoy contemporary Greek cuisine at the taverna and buy local produce, including wine, from the food store. The factory was originally built on the water so that the wine it produced could be pumped straight onto waiting ships. Now, it provides hotel guests with direct access to Kourouta beach and stunning views of the shimmering Ionian sea.

1. The guest rooms are located in old wine tanks overlooking a tranquil courtyard. The interiors are characterised by raw concrete and polished terrazzo.

2. Two steel drums stand in a meditative pool in the courtyard. Concrete slabs cut out to make doorways in the wine tanks now serve as large stepping stones.

3. Terrazzo used in the bathrooms mimics the tone of beach-pebble aggregates revealed wherever the former factory's old walls have been sliced through.

4. Each room has a double bed and a sofa that can serve as a single. Black metal pipes form hanging rails and frame the bathroom behind textured glass.

GET THE LOOK

BLACK FRAMEWORKS

Smart black metal-framed furniture suits any monochromatic interior and defines
sophisticated spaces. Open structures are ideal for minimalist schemes and clean black
lines complement heritage industrial features such as exposed brickwork and plaster.

1

SELECT SLEEK SEATING WITH INDUSTRIAL FLAIR
In this atmospheric space conceived by Warehouse Home, the black pedestal table is accompanied by an Officina dining chair. The sculptural chair was created by designer brothers Ronan and Erwan Bouroullec for Magis. It is characterised by a forged iron frame, powder-coated black, bolted to a geometric black plywood back and seat. The contrast between the forged and refined elements is effective and the chair is perfect for this modern home in a listed warehouse conversion.

2

OPT FOR A MODERN FOUR-POSTER BED DESIGN
This king-size iron canopy bed immediately brings the elegance and ambience of a boutique hotel to any bedroom. The pared-back linear outline updates the classic four-poster and is at once contemporary and timeless. It frames the sleeping area while drawing attention to any notable architectural features, like a high ceiling. The bed, available from Rockett St George, looks equally inviting dressed with crisp white bedlinen or layered with luxurious bedding and blankets.

3

SEEK OUT STYLISH BLACK STORAGE SOLUTIONS
Ferm Living's chic furniture and homeware items exemplify the best of Danish design, authentic and functional yet often also avant-garde. The Haze vitrine cabinet combines a black metal framework with wired glass for a strong industrial look. The Pujo coat stand has such a handsome format that it works equally well in a hallway or serving as an open wardrobe in a guest bedroom. The two over-sized spheres are striking but also serve a practical purpose for hanging hats.

2.

71 Nyhavn Hotel

CHARACTERFUL CONVERTED SPICE WAREHOUSES

In the heart of historic Copenhagen are two of the city's most well-preserved heritage buildings. The yellow warehouse dates back to 1830, while the red warehouse, which is protected, was constructed in 1804. They originally formed a single building, but its two wealthy spice merchant owners split it in two after falling out and flipping a coin. So, today the two converted warehouses are connected only on the ground floor, by the welcoming lobby of 71 Nyhavn. This charming boutique hotel is set on the sunny waterfront, at the corner of the photogenic Nyhavn canal and Copenhagen harbour. Externally, the brick façades remain virtually unchanged. Inside, the warehouses have undergone a sensitive renovation programme to provide high-end accommodation while still relaying the historic character of the property. Substantial Pomeranian pine beams and

pillars clearly display their age and bear evidence of the warehouses' many years of commercial use. It is almost possible to imagine the thick aroma of exotic spices that once hung in the air. These dark original timbers are cleverly juxtaposed throughout the hotel with contemporary Danish design additions, most crafted from light oiled oak which contrasts beautifully with the aged pine. In fact, the hotel serves many lessons in the effective layering of different timbers, old and new, and proves that an abundance of wooden surfaces and furniture can be incredibly striking. Bright white walls ensure the spaces feel light and spacious. 71 Nyhavn is an especially convenient base for exploring Copenhagen's many historic and cultural sights. But this delightful hotel also offers a captivating first-hand experience of the city's maritime and industrial past and a direct insight into Copenhagen's deserved renown as an international design destination.

1. The thick old plaster walls of 71 Nyhavn's lobby are decorated with paintings by prominent Danish painters. They include select works by Jens Jørgen Thorsen, Asger Jorn and other members of the twentieth-century avant-garde Cobra movement.

2. The original warehouses are over 200 years old. The yellow and red brickwork of the photogenic old buildings has been perfectly preserved and the green-painted wooden window shutters add to the historic character of the boutique waterfront hotel.

3. Breakfast is served in the old warehouse cellar, which was once used to store imported goods. The elegant CH20 Elbow Chair by Hans J. Wegner, from Carl Hansen & Son, is a recognisable Danish design. The chair is stackable, making it a practical choice, but its elegant oak frame also contrasts beautifully with the abundant historic timbers too.

4. 71 Nyhavn's 130 guest rooms feature gnarly old wooden beams, offset by light timber floors and modern Danish furniture. The sumptuous beds are by Carpe Diem. The bright Junior Suites located in the yellow warehouse are set over two floors, with a staircase. This suite includes a sculptural Fly sofa by Space Copenhagen, from &Tradition.

5. Aged timber beams even appear in the guest rooms' bright contemporary ensuite bathrooms. Black-framed bathroom furniture contrasts with gold fittings and sleek white tiling for an up-to-the-minute look that maximises the sense of space even in the more compact bathrooms. The toiletries are from indulgent Danish skin-care brand Karmameju.

6. This suite has an inviting mezzanine living and study area. At the desk is an oak Grand Prix chair, designed by Arne Jacobsen and available from Fritz Hansen. Its graphic form suits the geometry of the attic-like space. The Arne Jacobsen Swan sofa, upholstered in supple brown leather, is paired with a black occasional table from OXDENMARQ

GET THE LOOK

LIGHT TIMBER

Light wood furniture can soften an industrial-style interior and complements laid-back looks. Scandinavian pieces, beautifully crafted and with simple lines, suit old and new spaces. Meanwhile, design classics are being remade in pale timber for modern-day homes.

1 SELECT FURNITURE INSPIRED BY THE WORKSHOP

The Arco desk by Design House Stockholm combines the best of Scandinavian craftsmanship and industrial influences. It features a glass top, fixed to a pair of workbench-inspired oak trestles. The contents of the simple central drawer will be visible through the desktop, meaning the piece also serves as a form of display case. The Step stepladder by Design House Stockholm is as attractive as it is practical and can be hung decoratively on the wall, while Step Mini doubles up as a chair.

3 INVEST IN QUIRKY CONTEMPORARY LIGHTING

Industrial scissor light designs were originally conceived as a means of saving workspace in factory settings, the extendable arms pulled out and retracted as required. An ability to adjust lighting to suit every situation is just as appealing for a modern home. These wooden variants are the best by a long stretch, successfully reimagining classic lighting as pieces of modern wood craft. The playful Finnieston floor lamp was created by Samuel Chan, founder of Channels.

2 OPT FOR UNDERSTATED SHELVING SOLUTIONS

The Slow Shelf was created by Space Copenhagen for Stellar Works. The shelving system was designed as a companion to a chair conceived for the industrial chic setting of 108 Restaurant in Copenhagen, sister outlet to world-famous eatery NOMA. The elegant piece has a no-nonsense silhouette, combining Scandinavian and Japanese influences. But the form also calls to mind vintage bakers' units, with racked shelves. The simple, functional design is available in four different sizes and in a selection of different oak finishes, as well as natural or soap-finished walnut. The shelf is an attractive way to store favourite items.

4 CHOOSE A DESIGN ICON

Celebrating the 75th anniversary of the iconic aluminium original, Emeco released this white oak version of the 1006 Navy Chair. The Navy Wood Chair has the same smooth finish and simple form as its counterpart, but the timber brings an additional warmth that makes it suitable for industrial and traditional interiors alike. The chairs are also available in black stained oak and walnut, all handcrafted by expert Amish woodworkers in Pennsylvania.

2.

The Zetter

A VICTORIAN WAREHOUSE IN A VIBRANT QUARTER OF LONDON

There are more creative businesses per square mile in Clerkenwell than anywhere else in the world. Studios and showrooms for artists, designers and architects sit along Clerkenwell's quiet cobbled backstreets, amongst hidden gardens, historic churches and an array of pubs and restaurants. And here, in one of London's most appealing neighbourhoods, is an award-winning and independently owned boutique hotel. The Victorian warehouse was sensitively converted by The Zetter Group, and the eco-conscious hoteliers ensured that reclamation and the reuse of architectural salvage were at the heart of the transformation. Sustainable timber was used throughout the hotel. Original sash windows were retained. Chetwoods Architects conceived a five-storey atrium through the centre of the warehouse, with guest rooms wrapping around it and accessed by walkways overlooking the light-filled interior void. The guest room interiors, by London-based Precious McBane, contrast old and new elements, including restored vintage furniture upholstered in retro-style prints. Locally-sourced amenities include East London Gin and Hoxton Mini Press books. There are also seven rooftop rooms, benefitting from private terraces and panoramic London views. The circular, split-level Rooftop Deluxe features a curved patio and open-air bathtub. On sunny days, the ground-floor restaurant offers al fresco dining beside the cobbles, overlooked by Georgian townhouses. The Zetter is ideally situated for all of central London's major sights and well-connected for the West End and East London. But this intimate hotel is more than just a city base. It captures the creative spirit and the architectural richness of Clerkenwell, both past and present. The Zetter's charm and authenticity make it a design destination in itself.

1. The Zetter's location, in the heart of the historic and creative Clerkenwell district, can be enjoyed from the Juliet balconies of several of the rooms. With comfortable vintage chairs, this is the perfect spot to soak up the local atmosphere. Loading-style doors are a reminder of the old warehouse's past.

2. The exterior of the yellow-brick building has been painstakingly restored and retains its heritage character. The largely unaltered façade belies some of the modern interventions made to the interior and the quirky and eclectic decorative details that were introduced by design studio Precious McBane.

3. The Zetter hosts a rotating programme of new as well as established artists in the hotel's atrium, the artworks and sculptures changing every six weeks. Clusters of intimate seating arrangements in velvet and vibrant shades offset these works and the converted warehouse's whitewashed brick walls.

4. The guest rooms were all individually designed. They offer style, comfort and personality and most have plush carpeting. Retro lighting, such as this Jieldé floor lamp in red, floral upholstery and bright Zetter bedspreads in orange, blue, pink or green, all bring splashes of colour to the schemes.

5. Old botanical prints in many of the guest rooms complement the select items of industrial-style and vintage furniture. In this room, a simple wood and pipework hanging rail and shelf system sits beside a retro wooden desk, which is paired with a vintage plywood chair that has compass-shaped metal legs.

REAL HOME

VINTAGE FURNITURE

Combining old and new decorative elements creates the sensation of a scheme that has evolved over time. It is an approach well-suited to homes in heritage conversions. And sourcing and refurbishing vintage furniture offers an exciting opportunity for creativity.

TAKE INSPIRATION FROM THIS CHARACTER-RICH HOME

Actor Russell Tovey lives in a converted warehouse in Shoreditch, London.
Dating from the 1880s, the building once stored the textiles collections of
the British Museum, and that history has clearly inspired Tovey's approach
to his home. An avid collector with a strong eye for design, he designed the
apartment himself. In the open living-dining space, handmade pottery and
curios sourced from flea markets mix with refurbished furniture and pieces
by Charlotte Perriand and Matthew Hilton. Contemporary artworks by
famous names like Tracey Emin sit alongside pieces by new and emerging
artists (Tovey presents the hugely popular Talk Art podcast with his gallerist
friend Robert Diament). An area under the breakfast bar has been jazzed
up with a wallpaper by artist Jonas Wood. In the master bedroom stands a
modern bath on timber plinths with an industrial pipe-style filler. Beside it
is a design-classic chair by Gerrit Rietveld and vase by Shio Kusaka. The
mid-century chair nearby was reupholstered in a Raf Simons for Kvadrat
fabric. Fittingly, an array of tactile textiles complete Tovey's distinctive home.

Bangkok Publishing Residence

A PRESERVED PRINTING HOUSE THAT COMBINES ACCOMMODATION WITH A MUSEUM

Following a seven-year renovation, this former printing house opened in 2016 as an intimate bed-and-breakfast. The shophouse property was originally the family home of an independent publisher and the birthplace of the renowned *Bangkok Weekly* magazine. It has now been lovingly restored by the entrepreneurial publisher's granddaughter, Panida Oum Tosnaitada. Now, stepping inside Bangkok Publishing Residence from the busy Lan Luang Road, visitors are suddenly transported back to the mid-twentieth century and the heyday of Thailand's publishing industry. In addition to the restoration of the building itself, almost all of the furniture came from the old factory. The ground-floor lobby features lightly distressed leather seating, salvaged metal filing cabinets and even a recreation of Tosnaitada's grandfather's desk, complete with his old typewriter and pens.

There are shelves of leather-bound *Bangkok Weekly* magazine back issues. The space is filled with antique printing blocks, typesetting sorts and an array of other publishing memorabilia from the family archives. As the residence does not have a restaurant or a pool, the experience is more akin to attending a private house party. There are board games and a piano for guests to play in the lobby and impromptu jams and concerts occasionally take place. There are just eight individually designed and well-appointed bedrooms, each with antique furniture and wood-panelled walls. They are inviting places to retire after a day exploring bustling Bangkok. In fact, it is clear that Bangkok Publishing Residence offers a very different way to experience life in this modern-day metropolis. Set on the edge of Bangkok's Old City, the captivating bed-and-breakfast exudes Old World charm and gives a personal insight into the Thai capital's past.

1.& 2. With original walls and floors removed up to the fourth floor, the hotel lobby has an atrium-like appearance. The ground-floor space doubles as a museum, with an old print press, magazine covers and family collectables on display. The metal lift is new, but perfectly in keeping with the old building.

3.& 4. The eight individually designed guest suites feature antique furniture and exude an exotic Old World charm. Wood-panelled walls, painted cream or grey-blue, lighten the overall look, offsetting the dark wood floors and furniture. Modern amenities, such as the radios, were selected for their retro style.

5. In this master suite, a glazed panel with frosted glass serves as an attractive room divider while also creating privacy for the bedroom area. The feature has an understated industrial edge that suits the building's printing house past and calls to mind the unique mechanical ironwork lift in the hotel lobby.

5.

GET THE LOOK

VINTAGE CURIOS

From salvaged industrial moulds and unusual machinery parts to old signage, there are innumerable ways to honour and celebrate the past. But vintage displays can also signal personal passions and include cherished family heirlooms while injecting character into the home.

1 USE SOLID MANUFACTURING MOULDS AS INTRIGUING ART

These mid-twentieth-century moulds were salvaged by LASSCO from an English foundry that specialised in parts for aviation and military manufacturers. The hardwood moulds have been cleaned and mounted on reclaimed oak slabs. They have an abstract quality and still bear the notes and markings made by the foundry workers during the casting process. Displayed individually or in a group, the solid pieces will serve as eye-catching sculptural artworks on a console table while paying tribute to industrial craftsmanship.

2 DISPLAY AN INDUSTRIAL POSTER AS AN ARTWORK

This fascinating engineering poster is one of a set sourced by vintage experts Merchant & Found from an old engineering workshop in the Czech Republic. The poster depicts a series of technical industrial drawings that explain the process of sand casting and forming the wooden plugs used for creating cast metal parts. Whether mounted or left unframed, this delicately coloured and intricate paper placard will serve as a unique piece of wall art in any room of the home. Metal bulldog clips are a suitably industrial-style hanging solution.

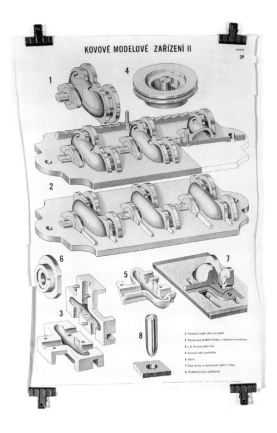

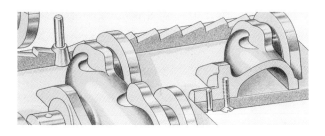

3 FIND PRACTICAL VINTAGE DECORATIVE ITEMS

English Salvage rescues these old teak brick moulds (top) from India. The boxes feature metal banding and different lettering and numbers. They are as characterful as they are functional, whether holding cutlery in the centre of a table or pencils on a desktop. These aluminium 1950s factory shoe forms (bottom) are available from Merchant & Found. The cast metal lasts are much less common than their wooden counterparts. They will look equally attractive arranged in a line along a shelf or put to work as unconventional bookends or doorstops.

Lighting

Good lighting is crucial in interior design. It is an often underestimated tool that actually has the power to transform a home. Different spaces will require alternative strategies and selections, and any areas with lower levels of natural light will pose a particular challenge. In addition to general lighting solutions for a room, careful attention should be paid to illuminating special architectural features, hero furniture and favourite decorative items or artworks. Time should be invested in picking the perfect pendant or chandelier and on the placement of table and floor lamps, bringing soothing warmth and ambience. In addition to their illuminating properties, the right lighting designs have the potential to not only complete a stylish scheme, but to elevate it. Oversized vintage pendants bring undeniable wow-factor, while upcycled creations are distinctive and intriguing, and bare bulbs create a strong utilitarian look. The options for decorative lighting are limitless.

Wilder, at Boundary hotel in London, celebrates the best of British produce throughout its dishes. And the interior detailing of the restaurant and bar, which is situated in the high-ceilinged basement of the converted warehouse hotel, also befits the menu's foraging theme. The spaces were designed by architecture studio Kirkwood McCarthy and include pendant lights imaginatively woven with tree branches, grasses and wildflowers.

The Robey

ART DECO MEETS INDUSTRIAL IN A CHICAGO HOTSPOT

Occupying two landmark buildings in Chicago's Wicker Park neighbourhood is one of the city's trendiest hotels. These two properties are noticeably different. North Tower is a soaring Art Deco skyscraper originally built in 1929 as an office building. The adjoining structure, once the Hollander Fireproof Warehouse, is a monument to The Second City's industrial era. Boutique hotel operator Grupo Habita first enlisted two Belgian practices, Nicolas Schuybroek Architects and Marc Merckx Interiors, to realise The Robey. The look is cool and industrial throughout, with vintage twists. Touches of brass and marble walls are nods to the Roaring Twenties and complement the Art Deco style lift doors. Terrazzo floors contrast with mid-century furniture. Low sofas in the Up Room indoor-outdoor rooftop bar invite visitors to linger and admire the panoramic city views. The 69 principal guest rooms are sparsely furnished. The aesthetic is moody and utilitarian and somewhat reminiscent of Mad Men style 1950s offices, with frosted glass and retro corded telephones. If the superb city views are too distracting at bedtime, motorised blackout panels lower over the windows. In the former fireproof warehouse, there are a further 20 Annex Loft rooms by French design studios Ciguë and Delordinaire, some of which sleep four in smart modern bunk beds and are ideal for larger parties. The Robey sits on the bustling crossing of Damen and Milwaukee Avenues, where the cool Wicker Park and Bucktown neighbourhoods meet and bookshops, vintage stores and boutiques abound. The hotel is also just over three miles to The Loop, the heart of Chicago. There are complimentary bikes for guests to explore the local area, but they will want to leave plenty of time to soak up the amenities and atmosphere at The Robey too.

1. The Paris and Montreal-based design practice Delordinaire was commissioned to design the hotel café, situated in the converted Hollander Fireproof Warehouse. The pared-back aesthetic encourages locals and guests to mingle in an informal setting. The 27-feet-long timber workbench incorporates the café at one end, serving freshly-brewed coffee, and at the other a casual co-working area with stools.

2. One of the two adjoining buildings that house The Robey was originally a fireproof warehouse. It houses 20 loft-style rooms and is widely regarded as the hip sibling of the more sophisticated larger portion of the hotel, set in the 1920s North Tower skyscraper. The hybrid of interior styles across The Robey's public spaces and rooms reflects Chicago's rich history and role as the crossroads of America.

3. The industrial-style ground floor guest area was conceived by the design team at Delordinaire as a 'programmable platform'. Leather banquettes and easy chairs create intimate clusters of seating and the high-ceilinged space with exposed concrete walls is illuminated by strip lights and bare bulbs. The minimalist setting is highly adaptable and is often used for seasonal stalls, concerts and activities.

3.

5.

6.

4. The 20 Annex Loft rooms are an affordable yet stylish solution for larger parties. Set in the former Hollander Fireproof Warehouse, with 11-feet-high ceilings and raw brick, they feature birch plywood and black steel bunk beds illuminated by industrial chic wall-hung Schoolhouse Electric bedside lamps.

5. The guest bedrooms are filled with natural light. The triangular-shaped Corner Suites offer the best views of the city skyline, with windows along two sides. Ensuring the guests' attention remains on the panoramic vistas, the rooms' furnishing is minimal, in black and slate grey with just splashes of ruby red.

6. The monochromatic bathrooms also display a pared-back approach, with understated industrial influences. Frosted wire-glass partition windows and doors provide both privacy and light. Chrome fixtures and faucets and plain white walls complete a functional, crisp and modern bathroom scheme.

GET THE LOOK

BARE BULBS

Whether hung in clusters or used individually, one of the easiest ways to achieve a utilitarian aesthetic is with bare bulb lighting. Filament bulbs create a vintage look, while there are oversized and ornate cut-glass alternatives for contemporary interior schemes.

1 SUSPEND A LINE OF BULBS AS A STYLISH FEATURE

A simple metal pole or frame can be looped with flex to support a selection of bare bulb lights. Hanging the bulbs at different heights and using bulbs of different sizes achieves an informal look. This is a stylish and cost-effective lighting solution that is particularly well-suited to casting light over a long worksurface or island in a kitchen. It can also be utilised in a bathroom, as in the industrial chic Los Angeles home of actress Diane Keaton (above), where bare bulbs illuminate a concrete basin.

2 CHANNEL INDUSTRIAL LUXE USING CUT GLASS

The Crystal Bulb by the British designer Lee Broom combines industrial influences with the delicate craftsmanship of crystal cutting. Each lead Crystal Bulb is handcrafted using traditional techniques, displaying a classic pattern inspired by old whisky glasses and decanters. The stunning ornamental design is available as a single pendant or with a chandelier fitting, with brushed brass or polished chrome holders. It will elevate the interiors of heritage and new homes alike.

4 CONSIDER AGED AND NEW METALLIC FINISHES

This industrial wall light by Old School Electric, available from Holloways of Ludlow, is a versatile solution for any home. Utilitarian and functional, it comes in classic finishes such as polished nickel and antique brass, as well as smart black and assorted bright colours for a more fun, modern effect. A row of industrial wall lights in a hallway or kitchen will form an attractive feature, but single lights also work well for bedsides and illuminating darker nooks.

3 MIX BARE BULBS WITH COLOURFUL FIXTURES

The E27 pendant light by Muuto is available in a wide array of colourful finishes. A naked LED bulb is held within a coloured rubber structure, providing a quirky material contrast and a light that is at once classic and contemporary, simple yet full of character. The bulb holder can be selected to complement a colour scheme. A group of different-coloured pendants hung together will look playful and appealing. A popular choice for children's rooms and for the young at heart.

5 FIND A SIMPLE SOLUTION FOR BEDSIDE TABLES

The Control Table Lamp mixes industrial and Scandinavian influences in an understated design that is ideal for side tables as well as work areas and small spaces. It was conceived for Muuto by the Stockholm-based design and architecture practice TAF Studio, who distilled the table lamp into its component parts, with an oversized Hi-Fi style dial and a bare bulb, presented on a plain display board. Turning the dial switches the lamp on and off and also adjusts its brightness.

The Steam Hotel

A FORMER POWER PLANT IN SWEDEN WITH A DISTINCTIVE SPA

As its name suggests, The Steam Hotel is situated within a former steam power plant. Located in Västerås, in central Sweden, the 18-storey building dates from 1917 and provided power for large swathes of the country until it ceased operation in 1982. Today, the towering structure on the edge of Lake Mälaren is a compelling example of adaptive reuse. The hotel was the brainchild of Sweden's Ess Group, who enlisted the services of Gothenburg-based design practice Spik Studios. Externally, the energy station's monolithic appearance was largely unchanged, while the interiors are a revelation. Ess Group retained as many original elements as possible. Colossal steel beams were left in the lobby, where they form a soaring structure around an open fireplace and copper chimney. Steam pipes run adjacent to aged timbers. An old steam boiler and fire trench now form a bar.

On the hotel's seventh floor, there is another direct reference to the building's past in the 800-square-metre club and indoor pool, which is heated by an old steam turbine salvaged from the plant. Throughout the property, these restored industrial features are offset by luxurious decorative additions, including glistening chandeliers which hang alongside modern wall lights and pendants by Mullan Lighting. The 264 bedrooms channel what is described by the hotel as an industrial-romantic aesthetic. The leaded factory windows, exposed brick and rough concrete surfaces contrast with the plump velvet-upholstered armchairs and bold floral prints. Just 50 minutes from Sweden's capital and creative heart, Stockholm, Ess Group has triumphantly transformed a defunct energy station into a design destination in its own right. In addition to The Steam Hotel's superb amenities, its interior décor is another powerful enticement to visit.

3.

1.& 2. The Chamberlin Grill is situated on the ground floor of The Steam Hotel. An enormous crystal chandelier and island bench seating make the most of the space's dramatic proportions. A mezzanine lounge and bar area above invites guests to sink into its plush velvet sofas with a drink.

3. In this suite, an industrial-style unit serves as an effective room divider, acting as the headboard for the bed as well as providing storage and shelving for the open-plan living area behind. A floral sofa is a pretty counterpoint to the room's raw concrete ceiling, exposed brick surfaces and metal trusswork.

4. The guest bedrooms feature bespoke cabinetry that combines aged brass frameworks with timber shelving and mesh-fronted cupboards. The open format of the units ensures that the textural quality of the bare concrete walls can still be appreciated. Cloche-style table lamps illuminate the desktops.

5. In the bathrooms, the showers and black metal vanity units and towel rails echo the power plant's leaded floor-to-ceiling windows. Lightly distressed tin-clad ceilings contrast strikingly with black and white floor tiles and polished marble surfaces. The touches of brass complete the industrial luxe look.

5.

CHANDELIERS

The word 'chandelier' brings to mind elaborate antique lighting adorned with glistening crystals. But there are a growing number of contemporary chandeliers that are ideally suited to industrial schemes and will draw attention to high ceilings and original features.

1 **ADOPT A MORE ARTISTIC APPROACH TO LIGHTING**
This 1,500-square-feet loft apartment is located in one of Tribeca's most attractive turn-of-the-century masonry buildings. Restored original timbers, exposed brick walls and new millwork, including custom joinery in zinc and oak, complete a scheme honouring the building's past while also creating a chic modern home. Workstead design studio was responsible for the property's remodel and suspended an elegant sculptural brass and bare bulb industrial chandelier over the dining table.

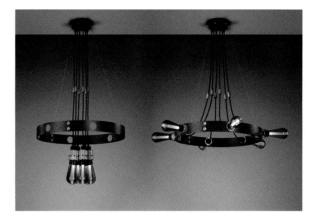

3 **CHOOSE AN ADJUSTABLE AND MODERN DESIGN**
The appropriately named Hero light by Buster + Punch offers two chandelier solutions in one, either of which will command attention in any setting. The six bare bulb pendant lights can be suspended vertically, providing more focused illumination, or fixed into the holes in the chandelier's ring. The Hero chandelier can be customised with a choice of two ring finishes and three metal options, as well as a choice of designer LED Buster Bulbs, which give an ambient glow.

2 **OPT FOR A MINIMALIST AND GEOMETRIC LIGHT**
The Wireflow Chandelier, designed by Arik Levy for Vibia, is a striking reinterpretation of the traditional chandelier form. The intricate three-dimensional supporting structure is formed from thin black electrical cables and completed with LED terminals. The futuristic design is at once simple yet intricate and has a transparency as well as a strong presence. The Wireflow is available in various different formulations, but can also be adapted to a customer's specific requirements.

4 **HANG A CHARACTERFUL UPCYCLED CREATION**
Los Angeles-based artist Carolina Fontoura Alzaga, founder of Facaro, creates remarkable modern-day chandeliers using recycled bicycle chains. The Connect series includes several different designs, but Facaro also takes special commissions. Discarded bike chains and rims are painstakingly cleaned and transformed into cascading chandeliers, table lamps and sconces. After degreasing, bike chains are left unfinished and display their patina and character to full effect.

Boundary London

A VICTORIAN WAREHOUSE CONVERSION BY A BRITISH DESIGN GIANT

his boutique bolthole is set in the heart of London's trendy Shoreditch, with an array of galleries, design shops, restaurants and bars right on its doorstep. But Boundary London also has two great restaurants of its own, together with two bars and, on the ground floor, a café, bakery and deli. The principal attraction for most visitors, however, is the hotel's design credentials. Boundary London is housed in a converted Victorian warehouse and former printing factory. The attractive red-brick building was sensitively restored by Conran & Partners, under the watchful eye of the visionary late Sir Terence Conran. A dramatic two-storey glass, steel and copper extension crowns the heritage structure and is topped by a rooftop bar and grill that offers impressive views over London. The interiors too are a celebration of old and new. There are bare brick walls and timber

floors, complemented by industrial lighting. The 17 individually decorated guest rooms are each dedicated to a twentieth-century design leader or movement. Instantly-recognisable iconic items of furniture and lighting abound. A Barcelona chair by Mies van der Rohe features in the room bearing the designer's name. The Josef Hoffmann room is fittingly decorated with geometric patterns. And further rooms pay homage to Bauhaus, Le Corbusier and Eileen Gray. The customised room treatments honour the key figures that influenced Sir Terence Conran in his long and celebrated career. But the approach also demonstrates the versatility of a warehouse conversion and proves that industrial features can be mixed with, even enhanced by, a variety of decorative styles. The old warehouse successfully repositioned its neighbourhood as a London hotspot, but the real excitement lies just beyond its lobby and in its rooms.

1. Wilder restaurant and bar is devoted to serving the best British produce. Foliage-woven lighting, sisal rugs and ash furniture subtly reference this theme. Earth-like natural plaster walls also suit the underground space and the bare original brickwork.

2. Boundary London is set in a reworked Victorian warehouse. It was painstakingly renovated by the famed British designer, architect and restaurateur Sir Terence Conran and first opened in 2009. The rooftop bar offers panoramic views over London.

3. In the guest rooms, bright white walls maximise natural light and draw attention to the exposed brick columns that frame the large windows. Each room has been individually decorated to reflect a different design style, with a customised headboard.

4. One of the rooms is dedicated to French interior and product designer Andrée Putman. She ran a business that produced notable twentieth-century homewares, including the supersized Felix Aublet floor lamp that stands on display in this bedroom.

REAL HOME

OVERSIZED LIGHTING

Supersize lights are an effective way to draw attention to dramatic proportions and original features. Suspending enormous pendants will highlight high ceilings and define open-plan living spaces. Vintage factory lighting will complement old timber and brick.

TAKE DESIGN INSPIRATION FROM THE INDUSTRIAL CHIC LOS ANGELES HOME OF A FAMOUS HOLLYWOOD ACTRESS

The Oscar-winning actress Diane Keaton has a keen eye for architecture and interior design and has renovated, lived in and sold a number of Los Angeles homes. Her current abode is a 9,000-square-feet industrial-style home in the Sullivan Canyon neighbourhood. Keaton details the property's transformation in her beautiful book 'The House That Pinterest Built' and confirms the platform was a direct source of décor ideas. She designed the modern-rustic-meets-industrial-chic home herself, in collaboration with the architect David Takacs and with designers Stephen Shadley and Cynthia Carlson. The concepts of factories, barns and compounds all provided key inspiration for the custom-designed building. The living area and kitchen feature light grey wooden floorboards, offsetting aged timber beams overhead. Exposed brick walls have been whitewashed to maximise natural light, while others remain bare to enhance the industrial qualities of the home. Enormous salvaged factory lights provide illumination throughout.

The Old Clare

A BOUTIQUE HOTEL WITH A RICH BREWING HISTORY

This urban bolthole is situated in Chippendale, an inner-city suburb of Sydney. It is set in the former Carlton and United Breweries Administration Building, dating from 1915, and what was once The County Clare, a 1940s pub. The Surry Hills-based practice Tonkin Zulaikha Greer Architects was responsible for the transformation of the two adjoining buildings into The Old Clare hotel. The architects linked the heritage-listed properties by enclosing a former laneway and adding a striking glass rooftop extension that includes an inviting swimming pool and bar. Much of the raw architectural fabric has been left exposed, while the new interventions subtly reference the historic buildings. The rectangular and square panes of a new glass atrium mimic the window shapes of the two older properties. Of the 69 guest rooms, no two are the same. The Showroom Suite features a timber bar salvaged from the former brewery building, while the vast C.U.B. Suite is located in the intact panelled boardroom and the Chippendale Loft is set over two levels. Many of the rooms benefit from exposed brickwork and plaster walls, as well as original timber window frames. Colour is used sparingly and in splashes to bring the older textures and tones to life. There is a distinctive buzz about Chippendale, an up-and-coming creative neighbourhood filled with art galleries, design studios, chic cafés and restaurants. The Old Clare also has plenty to offer locals and travellers alike. The two bars honour the hotel's long brewing connections. The hybrid décor throughout the three restaurants and guest bedrooms successfully blends heritage and modern elements. The Old Clare has a fresh modern attitude and captures some of Chippendale's gritty past. It leaves all of its visitors feeling rested and inspired in equal measure.

1. The Old Clare is full of distinctive architectural features and celebrates the juxtaposition of new and old, polished and raw. Quirky vintage décor in the hotel's lobby includes a steampunk dentist's chair and an array of gig posters plastering the walls.

2. The architects enclosed and reactivated a once disused lane between the two original buildings. A four-storey glass atrium spans the laneway, creating a space that is at once public and private. It provides an attractive entranceway into The Old Clare hotel.

3. Exposed brickwork and plaster walls, blackbutt timber floors and preserved bare wooden window frames showcase the authentic character of the heritage buildings. Smart modern touches include timber cabinetry in the bedrooms and bathrooms.

4. Each bedroom features a different vintage chair from the personal collection of the hotel's owner, Singaporean hotelier and restaurateur Loh Lik Peng. Beirut-based lighting designers PSLab made the black steel and hand-blown glass pendant lights.

5. The soaring ceiling heights give every room a sense of spaciousness and grandeur, enhanced by enormous beds with oversized headboards and crisp white bedding. The rooms are also furnished sparingly, ensuring the older features still dominate.

5.

6. British designer-maker Paul Firbank, also known by his brand name The Rag And Bone Man, was commissioned to create over 100 upcycled pieces for the hotel. These included a desk lamp for every guest room, combining a vintage screw-jack base with a swivelling motorcycle engine cover as a shade.

"The magic of the hotel lies in its adaptive reuse. Points in history and processes in past construction are both captured and revealed."

TIM GREER
TONKIN ZULAIKHA GREER
ARCHITECTS

UPCYCLED LIGHTING

From supersized floor lamps to unusual and tactile pendants, designers around the world are creating distinctive lighting using salvaged and recycled materials. In addition to their sustainability credentials, these lights serve as original and memorable decorative features.

1
CELEBRATE LARGE-SCALE SUSTAINABLE STYLE

French designer Axel-Olivier Icard takes materials salvaged from manufacturing and industrial sites and transforms them into unique furniture and lighting. He recovers and recycles wood, leather, steel and even concrete, combining the elements into show-stopping pieces. One remarkable example of his work is a refurbished dentist's column from Sweden, which Icard has imaginatively converted into a substantial polished floor lamp that is full of quirky industrial character.

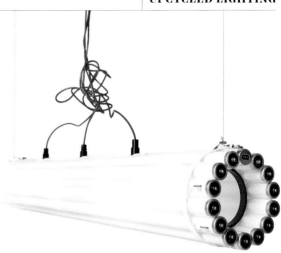

3
GIVE SPENT FILAMENTS A NEW LEASE OF LIFE

The Recycled Tube Light by Canadian lighting and furniture brand Castor Design is comprised of a bundle of burnt out fluorescent bulbs. These are held in a new cylindrical form by rubber strips and steel and lit from within using LEDs. The striking industrial-style light is available in various lengths, ranging from four to eight feet, and can be customised with red or black flex. The pendant provides ambient illumination and looks particularly impressive over a table.

2
CHOOSE AN INDUSTRIAL-STRENGTH FLOOR LAMP

This large adjustable floor-standing lamp can extend to over two metres in height. The movement of this sizeable floor lamp by Paul Firbank, The Rag and Bone Man, was based on luffing crane mechanisms. The shade is made from parts of a road sweeper, a brake drum and several components from a Pratt and Whitney jet engine. The base swivels on a large car wheel bearing, topped with parts saved from a 1920s scenic railway. Very much a case of go big and go home.

4
EMBRACE LIGHTING CRAFTED IN CARDBOARD

British designer Tabitha Bargh has always been passionate about creating unexpected homeware in recycled material. Her CartOn collection of sustainable light shades are hand-made, the layers of corrugated cardboard individually placed to establish a light and dark effect and fixed using a non toxic, bio-degradable glue. Several of the pendant shades adopt the recognisable form of classic factory lights, making them well-suited to industrial schemes.

1.

Vipp Chimney House

A HOME-FROM-HOME IN A FORMER WATER PUMPING STATION

Danish design brand Vipp has conceived an original way for its customers and fans to experience its products in a fully immersive setting. The original Vipp hotel, known as Shelter, opened in 2004, is a steel-clad forest cabin on the edge of a lake in southern Sweden. Meanwhile Vipp Loft is set above the Vipp headquarters in an old printing factory from 1910 in Copenhagen's Islands Brygge area. Each 'self-serve' hotel cleverly recreates the comfort, personality and ambience of a private home and is a compelling yet uncommercial environment within which to appreciate and test-drive Vipp products. Also in the city of Copenhagen is the Vipp Chimney House. A former water pumping station built in 1902 and featuring a towering chimney, it has a distinctive identity of its very own. Vipp collaborated with the internationally renowned Danish firm Studio David Thulstrup on

the restoration and rebirth of the heritage structure. The industrial character and charm of the architectural shell were painstakingly preserved. Once inside, however, guests find bright modern interiors brought to life with light grey render, custom-developed terrazzo floors and metal doors, and finished with cutting-edge fixtures and curated artworks. The house feels at once high-end and attainable. In addition to the fully-equipped open-plan black Vipp kitchen, there is an impressive dining area leading to a light-filled living space, two bathrooms and the two bedrooms on the new mezzanine. Throughout the house, there are striking Vipp lights, furniture and homeware products and, of course, the iconic Vipp pedal bin with which the brand launched 80 years ago. The Vipp Chimney House enables guests to check in to a historic landmark, but also to savour exceptional contemporary interiors and exemplary Danish designs.

4.

1. The dramatic steel staircase intersects the open-plan ground floor and serves as a divider between the Vipp kitchen and adjacent dining area and the principal living space. Its sleek contemporary form is clad in extruded aluminium panelling, which has a fine corrugated surface that reflects natural light.

2. The Vipp Chimney House honours, in its name, the former water pumping station's 35-metre-tall chimney. The distinctive minaret-shaped structure was added to the original 1902 building in 1928. It was restored as part of the property's year-long conversion and remains a landmark for the locality.

3. The two bedrooms, located on the first floor, have glass panels and overlook the atrium. The calm master bedroom further benefits from access to a private balcony via steel-framed glass doors. A light-weight yet opaque voile curtain can be drawn across the industrial-style black railing for privacy.

4. The atrium is almost nine metres in height, with a skylight offering a view up the neck of the soaring chimney. The dramatic void is accentuated by a trio of five-metre-long custom fabricated pendant lamps, with sandblasted Perspex discs and polished stainless steel poles, designed by Northern Lights.

PYLON LIGHTS

For wow-factor lighting with an industrial edge, there are vintage and contemporary designs based on insulator parts. Whether formed from salvaged glass or ceramic recreations, these pendants, floor lamps and sconces will all offer electrifying results.

1

ILLUMINATE INTERIORS WITH UPCYCLED LAMPS
Felix Lighting Specialists offer rare and wonderful lighting, much of it vintage or crafted from reclaimed elements. This eye-catching wall light incorporates a salvaged 1930s American electricity pylon insulator in green glass. The fitting includes the original heavy-duty cast-metal housing. In classic and contemporary schemes, this wall lamp offers an opportunity to create an impact and will emit a soft glow. It is particularly well-suited to an entrance hallway, where it will add drama.

2

SETTLE ON MODERN PYLON-INSPIRED LIGHTING
These eye-catching lights are all available from Holloways of Ludlow and are perfect for industrial environs. The matching Transmission floor lamp and oversized pendant by Lasvit are crafted from individual glass half-domes fused together with heat and supported by metal frameworks. The lamp is almost two metres in height, with a base reminiscent of soaring transmission towers. And the pendant also makes a bold statement due to both its size and composition.

3

SUSPEND STATEMENT CERAMIC PENDANT LIGHTS
Italian brand Toscot channels the manufacturing traditions of Tuscany in its designs. These Battersea lights, available from Holloways of Ludlow, were inspired by electrical isolators of the early nineteenth-century. The series is named after Battersea Power Station, London, and comes in various sizes and styles. The off-white 'oyster' ceramic shades achieve the look and feel of the original components and attention has even been paid to recreating the stamped serial numbers.

The Hoxton Paris

AN EIGHTEENTH CENTURY TOWNHOUSE AND FORMER CLOTHING FACTORY

The first French outpost for London-based The Hoxton hotel brand, The Hoxton Paris is situated in the second arrondissement and old garment district of the world's fashion capital. The eighteenth-century townhouse was once the home of Etienne Rivié, advisor to King Louis XV, but had more recently been used as a clothing factory. Classified as a 'monument historique', the building offered many attractive features which were carefully restored. Hotel owner Ennismore's in-house design team collaborated with Soho House on the design of the public spaces. The cobblestone-floored courtyard-style lobby has original iron columns and is decorated with tassel lamps and jewel-toned velvet sofas and armchairs. It also includes a Winter Garden with a living wall of foliage. These areas prove popular with guests as well as with local business people and Instagrammers. From the lobby, a 300-year-old spiral staircase ascends through five palatial floors of guest rooms. Conceived by Monaco-based design agency Humbert & Poyet, the rooms honour the building's history through their traditional cornicing, panelling and reclaimed oak chevron flooring. But laminates and industrial-style metal partition walls also inject contemporary style and reference French design greats Jean Prouvé and Mathieu Matégo. The iconic lighting of Bernard-Albin Gras is also on display. Each of the Hoxton hotels complements its surrounding neighbourhood. The Hoxton Paris is set in the heart of the city, just a stone's throw from the Louvre, Musée d'Orsay and Centre Pompidou. Arriving at this distinctive boutique hotel, and stepping beyond its Rococo façade, seasoned travellers, gourmands and art lovers will find plenty of creative inspiration. Here old meets new to the utmost success, with uniquely Parisian and Hoxton twists.

3.

1. Rivié restaurant offers traditional brasserie-style dining with timber panelling, which has been given a fresh modern update with distressed plaster walls, leather banquette seating and marble-topped bars. A large skylight illuminates the space by day, while glass globe pendants provide a warm evening glow.

2. Accommodation at The Hoxton Paris combines New York loft style with industrial flair and 1950s retro elements. Each of the 172 guest bedrooms features a small library of books recommended by Parisians, inviting guests to linger on longer in their stylish environs and soak up the flavour of the city.

3. Original oak flooring and beams remind guests of the building's heritage and are complemented by the Hoxton brand's trademark feature walls and dusky accent colours. The industrial-style bedside lighting is height-adjustable and was sourced from the leading French lighting brand DCW éditions.

"The room décor pays homage to two very important periods in Parisian history: the late 19th century and the 1950s."

ENNISMORE CREATIVE STUDIO

4. A frosted glass and metal factory-style dividing wall separates this guest bedroom and its ensuite bathroom. An integrated shelf with brass hanging rails is an ingenious use of the available space. The subtle utilitarian elements are complemented by the leather headboard with its smart strap detailing.

5. There are discernible industrial influences in the inviting and spacious bathrooms. The simple white subway tiles on the walls are offset by geometric floor tiles. Black metal-framed storage furniture and shower screens mix with aged copper cage lights, faucets and shower fittings to striking effect.

BEDROOM LIGHTING

Suitable bedroom lighting is essential for relaxation and a good night's sleep. But in addition to creating a tranquil ambience and providing focused illumination for bedtime reading, the right lamps will frame a bedhead and elevate a bedroom's design scheme.

1 INVEST IN THESE ICONIC AND ADJUSTABLE LAMPS

In 1921, Bernard-Albin Gras designed a series of lamps for use in offices and industrial environments. Subsequently known as Gras lamps, their form was simple, functional, robust and ergonomic. The design was truly original and ahead of its time; the twentieth-century's first articulated lamp. Le Corbusier was one of the series' earliest supporters and the lamps have only increased in popularity over the years. French company DCW éditions now produces the classic Gras lamps, alongside new collections of contemporary yet timeless lighting designs.

2 FIX A DOUBLE LIGHTING DESIGN ABOVE THE BED

Extending from a single wall fixture, the Double Lampe Gras by DCW éditions is available in various sizes and with the option to select different shade colours or finishes. The double lamp fitting is a useful solution for beds set into alcoves or with limited space either side and liberates room on bedside tables for favourite objects, photographs or artworks. The distinctive double-headed light will always serve as a stylish decorative feature above a bed, with or without a headboard.

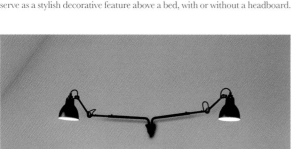

3 OPT FOR HEAVY-DUTY INDUSTRIAL-STYLE LAMPS

The architect Dominique Perrault collaborated with designer Gaëlle Lauriot-Prévost to create the In The Tube collection for DCW éditions. They were inspired by the industrial striplights commonly utilised in French power stations. The wall lamps are available in a range of lengths and diameters and can be fixed horizontally or vertically. Gold, copper or silver reflectors provide different types of light, from warm to cool, while an optional mesh over the bulb acts as a diffuser.

4 LOOK OUT FOR INTEGRATED READING LIGHTS

The practical and multifunctional Biny bedside light by DCW éditions has two integrated LEDs; one a directional spotlight, perfect for reading in bed, the other an LED plate set behind adjustable fins to provide diffused ambient light for the room. It also features a USB socket. The on/off switch cycles through the light functions, enabling users to set them on any combination to suit changing needs. Right and left orientations are available for use either side of the bed.

5 SELECT STYLISH AND SPACE-SAVING SOLUTIONS

Le Mobilier de Gras Plug and Dream by DCW éditions is a beautifully simple bedside table in steel, wood and rubber. The functional wall-mounted angled design is available as both left- and right-facing solutions to suit each side of the bed. Each cleverly incorporates an iconic N°216 Lampe Gras articulating light, with the option to select different lampshade colours to match an interior. The larger Plug and Play version is a smart work station for offices and homes.

DESIGN IN PRACTICE

Warehouse Home offers specialist services for homeowners seeking industrial-inspired interiors. Our experienced team can provide space plans and moodboards, design bespoke furniture, source vintage items and manage room makeovers or entire renovations.

This grade II listed former warehouse stands on one of the oldest streets in east London. Our team wanted to honour its original features and reflect the area's history. We designed haberdashery-style cabinets (1 and 2) to complement antique mahogany units in the dressing room. A bespoke headboard in Timorous Beasties' London Toile, with matching cushions and blinds, creates a chic guest room (5). Nineteenth-century metal shelving from Retrouvius acts as an open wardrobe (4). The master bedroom headboard (6) combines an oak frame and Zoffany's London 1832 map linen. In the double-height living room (3), Rakks shelves form an impressive library. House of Hackney's Caspar velvet and Rose Uniacke's jumbo corduroy were chosen for two sofa.com sofas set on a vintage Persian rug. Animal-print cushions reflect the owner's love of travel and refer to exotic goods once traded in the local docks.

Image Credits

Front Cover Chris Court **1** Dave Burk **2-3** Claus Brechenmacher and Reiner Baumann **4** Sophie Bush, photography Debbie Bragg; Section opener image credits, refer to relevant page numbers **6-7** Taggart Sorensen **8-9** Su Shengliang **10-13** Courtesy of Yangshuo Sugar House **15** Manchester show apartment by Warehouse Home, styling Olivia Gregory, photography Oliver Perrott **16-19** Tetsuya Ito **20-21** Claire Esparros **22-25** Courtesy of The Singular Patagonia **26-27** Eugeni Bach **28-33** Taggart Sorensen **34-35** Styling Lucy Gough, photography David Cleveland **36-39** Jonas Bjerre-Poulsen **40** Michael Sinclair **41** The Beldi by Chan and Eayrs, photography Taran Wilkhu; **42-45** Courtesy of Ovolo Hotels **46-47** Tom Bird **48-49** Pedro Pegenaute **50-51** Derryck Menere **53** Factory conversion set by Warehouse Home, styling Hannah Franklin, photography Oliver Perrott **54-59** Courtesy of Ennismore **60** Steel Vintage photography Chris Lucas **61** Steel Vintage photography Chris Lucas; Loftlight photography Marcin Petkowicz, courtesy of Darklight Design; Tonone photography Wonderwood Photography; Flos photography Piero Fasanotto, courtesy of Holloways of Ludlow **62-67** Claus Brechenmacher and Reiner Baumann **68** Nick Fraser photography James Champion **69** Residence HM by Lim + Lu, photography Nirut Benjabanpot; RF Apartment by Superlimão, photography Maira Acayaba **70-71** Courtesy of The Warehouse Hotel **72-77** Lauren Bamford **78-79** Adam Carter Photography **80-83** Spencer Lowell, courtesy of Trunk Archive **84** Will Ellis **85** Magic Egg Guesthouse by Jersey Ice Cream Co, photography Tara Mangini; EyeSwoon home office, photography Athena Calderone **86-89** Philipp Obkircher **90-91** Zoe Spawton **92** Dzek photography Angus Mill **93** Mandarin Stone photography Oli Douglas; Foresso photography Luke A. Walker **94-97** Courtesy of Armazém Luxury Housing **98** (From left) Panbeton® OSB by Terence Woodgate, Timber and Chevrons by Jean-Philippe Nuel, photography Lux Production; Vertical Planks by Studio LCDA, courtesy of Concrete LCDA **99** Lux Production **100-103** Courtesy of Ironworks Hotel Indy **104-105** Debbie Bragg **106-109** Sharyn Cairns **110** (Top) Sharyn Cairns; (Bottom) Tom Ross **111** Tom Ross **112** Styling Hannah Franklin, photography Oliver Perrott **113** Bedroom scheme by Warehouse Home, styling Hannah Bort, photography Beth Evans; (Top right) LinenMe photography Inga Lukauskiene **114-119** Dave Burk **120** Courtesy of Soho Home **121** (Left and top right) Styling Lucy Gough, photography Oliver Perrott; (Bottom right) Styling Hannah Franklin, photography Oliver Perrott **122-127** Courtesy of The Warehouse Hotel **128** FRED desk and Ginger chair by Roberto Lazzeroni for Poltrona Frau, courtesy of Poltrona Frau S.p.A **129** BY THORNAM photography Lars Ranek; Bethan Gray photography Julian Abrams; Dining space by Warehouse Home, styling Hannah Franklin, photography Oliver Perrott **130-131** Lyndon French **132-135** Spencer Lowell, courtesy of Trunk Archive **136** Ilan Rubin, courtesy of Trunk Archive **137** (Left) Bruno Augsburger; (Top right) Styling Rita Palanikumar, photography Simon Habegger; (Bottom right) Styling Lucy Gough, photography David Cleveland **138** Edmund Dabney **139** Nicholas Worley **140-141** Edmund Dabney **142-143** Nicholas Worley **144** Photoshoot Portugal **145** Moroso photography Alessandro Paderni; People's Industrial Design Office photography 51PHOTOS **146-147** Courtesy of Adjara Group **148-153** Romain Ricard **154-155** Greg Cox, courtesy of Bureaux **156-161** Rasmus Hjortshøj, courtesy of COAST Studio **162-163** Charlie Schuck **164-167** Courtesy of the Titanic Hotel **168-169** Anne-Catherine Scoffoni, courtesy of Image Professionals **170-173** Heidi's Bridge, courtesy of This Represents **174** Rory Gardiner **175** (Bottom left and right) Rory Gardiner **176-179** Michael Wee **180-181** Michael Moran, courtesy of OTTO **182-185** Nicholas Worley **186-187** Hey!Cheese **188-191** Courtesy of The Royal Portfolio **192-193** Marte Lundby Rekaa **194-197** Courtesy of Soho House **199** Pinch photography James Merrell, courtesy of Pinch **200-203** Courtesy of Adjara Group **204** Terzo Piano art direction and image production for Fiandre Architectural Surfaces **206-207** Michael Wee **208-213** Nicole Franzen **214-215** Simon Maxwell **216-219** Matthew Williams **222-225** Matthew Williams **226** Dan Funderburgh for Flavor Paper photography Boone Speed **227** The Monkey Puzzle photography Chris Leah, courtesy of Dowsing & Reynolds **228-231** Courtesy of The Collective Paper Factory **232-233** Kevin Kunstadt **234** Nicole England **235** Courtesy of Ovolo Hotels **236** Nicole England **237** (Top) Nicole England; (Bottom) Michael Wee **238** (Top) Nicole England; (Bottom) Michael Wee **239** Michael Wee **240** (Top) Shift 01 by Arik Levy for Savoir Beds photography Paul Raeside; (Bottom) Harlech 12 by Savoir Beds photography Dominic Blackmore **241** B Bed by Sacha Walckhoff for Savoir Beds photography Dominic Blackmore **242-245** Claus Brechenmacher & Reiner Baumann Photography **246** Dining scene by Warehouse Home, styling Hannah Franklin, photography Oliver Perrott **247** Left Courtesy of Rockett St George; (Right) Courtesy of Ferm Living **248-253** Courtesy of Arp-Hansen Hotel Group **255** (Left) Stellar Works photography courtesy of Nine United UK; (Top right) Channels photography Philip Vile **256-259** Darren Chung **260-261** Helen Cathcart, courtesy of Dillon & Friends **262-265** Courtesy of Bangkok Publishing Residence **266** Courtesy of LASSCO Three Pigeons **268-269** Courtesy of Boundary London **270-275** Adrian Gaut **276** (Left) Styling Linda Åhman, photography Anna Kern, courtesy of Image Professionals; (Right) Lisa Romerein, courtesy of OTTO (from the book *The House That Pinterest Built* by Diane Keaton, published by Rizzoli) **277** (Top right) Old School Electric photography courtesy of Holloways of Ludlow **278-283** Courtesy of The Steam Hotel **284** Matthew Williams **285** (Bottom right) Facaro photography Tod Seelie **286-289** Courtesy of Boundary London **290-291** Lisa Romerein, courtesy of OTTO (from the book *The House That Pinterest Built* by Diane Keaton, published by Rizzoli) **292** Nikki To **293** Chris Court **294** (Top) Chris Court; (Bottom) Nikki To **295** Chris Court **296-297** Nikki To **298** Axel-Olivier Icard **299** (Left) The Rag & Bone Man photography Damian Griffiths; (Top right) Castor Design photography Peter Andrew Lusztuk; (Bottom right) Tabitha Bargh photography Yeshen Venema **300-303** AM Studios **305** (Right) Toscot photography courtesy of Holloways of Ludlow **306-311** Alan Jensen **312** (Left) Ian Scigliuzzi; (Right) Marie Pierre Morel **313** (Top left) Ian Scigliuzzi; (Top right) Marie Pierre Morel; (Bottom left and right) Ian Scigliuzzi **314-315** Tarry + Perry Photography

Hotels

71 Nyhavn Hotel, 71nyhavnhotel.com
1051, Copenhagen, Denmark

Ace Hotel Chicago, acehotel.com
311 North Morgan Street, Chicago, Illinois, 60607, USA

Ace Hotel Downtown Los Angeles, acehotel.com
929 South Broadway, Los Angeles, California, 90015, USA

Armazém Luxury Housing, armazemporto.com
Rue de Miragaia 93, 4050-387, Porto, Portugal

Bangkok Publishing Residence, bpresidence.com
31-33-35-37-37/1 Lang Luang Road, Wat Sommanat, Pom Prap Sattru Phai, Bangkok, 10100, Thailand

Boundary London, boundary.london
2-4 Boundary Street, Shoreditch, London, E2 7DD, UK

Dexamenes, dexamenes.com
Kourouta Beach, Beach Front, Amaliada 272 00, Greece

Fabriken Furillen, furillen.com
Rute Furilden, 870 642 58, Lärbro, Sweden

Gorgeous George, gorgeousgeorge.co.za
118 St George's Mall, Cape Town, 8001, South Africa

Hotel Cycle, onomichi-u2.com
6-15 Nishigoshocho, Onomichi, Hiroshima 722-0037, Japan

Hotel Emma, thehotelemma.com
136 East Grayson Street, San Antonio, Texas, 78215, USA

Ironworks Hotel Indy, ironworkshotelindy.com
2721 East 86th Street, Indianapolis, Indiana, 46240, USA

Locke At Broken Wharf, lockeliving.com
Broken Wharf House, 2 Broken Wharf, London, EC4V 3DT, UK

Lokal, staylokal.com
139 North 3rd Street, Philadelphia, Pennsylvania, 19106, USA

Michelberger Hotel, michelbergerhotel.com
39-40 Warschauer Street, Berlin, 10243, Germany

Ovolo 1888 Darling Harbour, ovolohotels.com
139 Murray Street, Pyrmont, Sydney, New South Wales, 2009, Australia

Ovolo Southside, ovolohotels.com
64 Wong Chuk Hang Road, Southside, Hong Kong, China

Ovolo Woolloomooloo, ovolohotels.com
6 Cowper Wharf Roadway, Woolloomooloo, Sydney, New South Wales, 2011, Australia

Paramount House Hotel, paramounthousehotel.com
80 Commonwealth Street, Surry Hills, Sydney, New South Wales, 2010, Australia

Soho House Chicago, sohohouse.com
113-125 North Green Street, Chicago, Illinois, 60607, USA

Soho Warehouse, sohohouse.com
1000 South Santa Fe Avenue, Los Angeles, California, 90021, USA

Stamba Hotel, stambahotel.com
14 0108 Merab, Kostava Street, Tbilisi, Georgia

The Audo, theaudo.com
130 Århusgade, Copenhagen, 2150, Denmark

The Collective Paper Factory, thecollective.com
37-06 36th Street, Long Island City, New York, 11101, USA

The Eliza Jane, theelizajane.com
315 Magazine Street, New Orleans, Louisiana, 70130, USA

The Hoxton Paris, thehoxton.com
30-32 Rue de Sentier, Paris, 75002, France

The Hoxton Williamsburg, thehoxton.com/williamsburg
97 Wythe Avenue, Brooklyn, New York, 11249, USA

The Krane, thekrane.dk
1 Skudehavnsvej, København, 2100, Denmark

The Old Clare, theoldclarehotel.com
1 Kensington Street, Chippendale, Sydney, New South Wales, 2008, Australia

The Robey, therobey.com
2018 West North Avenue, Chicago, Illinois, 60647, USA

The Silo, theroyalportfolio.com
Silo Square, Victoria & Albert Waterfront, Cape Town, 8001, South Africa

The Singular Patagonia, thesingular.com
Km 5 4 Norte S/N, Puerto Natales, Chile

The Steam Hotel, steamhotel.se
Ångkraftsvägen 14, Västerås, 721 31, Sweden

The Warehouse Hotel, thewarehousehotel.com
320 Havelock Road, Robertson Quay, 169628, Singapore

The Waterhouse at South Bund,
1-3 Maojiayuan Road, Huangpu, Shanghai, 200010, China

The Zetter, thezetter.com
88 Clerkenwell Road, London, EC1M 5RJ, UK

Titanic Hotel, titanichotelliverpool.com
Regent Road, Liverpool, L3 0AN, UK

Veriu Broadway, veriu.com.au
35 Mountain Street, Ultimo, Sydney, New South Wales, 2007, Australia

Vipp Chimney House, vipp.com
Strandøre 5, 2100 København, Denmark

Whitworth Locke, lockeliving.com
74 Princess Street, Manchester, M1 6JD, UK

Wm. Mulherin's Sons, wmmulherinssons.com
1355 North Front Street, Philadelphia, Pennsylvania, 19122, USA

Wythe Hotel, wythehotel.com
80 Wythe Avenue, Brooklyn, New York, 11249, USA

Yangshuo Sugar House,
102 Dongling Road, Guilin, 541900, China

Architects/Designers

ADI Studio, adistudio.ie (Titanic Hotel, Liverpool, UK)

Alexander Owen Architecture, aoarchitecture.co.uk (Cleo's Place, London, UK)

Anna and Eugeni Bach, annaeugenibach.com (Chocolate Factory, La Bisbal, Spain)

Arcgency, arcgency.com (The Krane, Copenhagen, Denmark)

Asylum, theasylum.com.sg (The Warehouse Hotel, Singapore)

Becky Shea Design, beckyshea.com (Grand Street Loft, New York, USA)

Breathe Architecture, breathe.com.au (Paramount House Hotel, Sydney, Australia)

Büro Koray Duman, b-kd.com (Publisher's Loft, New York, USA)

Chan + Eayrs, chanandeayrs.com (New Cross Lofts, London, UK; The Beldi, London, UK)

Chetwoods Architects, chetwoods.com (The Zetter, London, UK)

Christopher Reeve, cpreeve.com (Bermondsey warehouse conversion, London, UK)

Ciguë, cigue.net (The Robey, Chicago, USA)

Commune Design, communedesign.com (Ace Hotel, Chicago, USA; Ace Hotel Downtown Los Angeles, USA)

Conran and Partners, conranandpartners.com (Boundary, London, UK)

Curate Design, curate-design.com (Ironworks Hotel Indy, Indianapolis, USA)

Cynthia Carlson Associates, cynthiacarlson.com (Diane Keaton's RRR House, Los Angeles, USA)

Darmody Architecture, darmodyarchitecture.com (Titanic Hotel, Liverpool, UK)

Delordinaire, delordinaire.com (The Robey, Chicago, USA)

Ennismore Design Studio, ennismore.com (The Hoxton Williamsburg, New York, USA)

Enrique Concha, enriqueconcha.com (The Singular Patagonia, Puerto Bories, Chile)

Feix & Merlin, feixandmerlin.com (De Havilland Loft, London, UK)

Fox Johnston, foxjohnston.com.au (Paramount House Hotel, Sydney, Australia)

Grzywinski+Pons, gp-arch.com (Locke Broken Wharf, London, UK; Whitworth Locke, Manchester, UK)

HAO Design, haodesign.tw (Starburst House, Beijing, China)

Hartshorne Plunkard Architecture, hparchitecture.com (Soho House Chicago, USA)

Hassell, hassellstudio.com (Ovolo Woolloomooloo, Sydney, Australia)

Heatherwick Studio, heatherwick.com (The Silo Hotel, Cape Town, South Africa)

Horizontal Design, cnhorizontal.com (Alila Yangshuo, Guilin, China)

Humber & Poyet, humbertpoyet.com (The Hoxton Paris, France)

Jersey Ice Cream Co, jerseyicecreamco.com (Lokal, Philadelphia, USA)

Jonathan Tuckey Design, jonathantuckey.com (Michelberger Hotel, Berlin, Germany)

JSA Studio, jsastudio.com.au (Veriu Broadway, Sydney, Australia)

Kirkwood McCarthy, kirkwoodmccarthy.com (Wilder at Boundary London, UK)

Klas Hyllén Architecture, klashyllen.com (The Vintner's Conversion, Bradford on Avon, UK)

KplusK Associates, kplusk.net (Ovolo Southside, Hong Kong, China)

K-Studio, k-studio.gr (Dexamenes, Kourouta, Greece)

Le Whit, lewhit.com (Pioneer Square Loft, Seattle, USA)

Lim + Lu, limandlu.com (Residence HM, Hong Kong, China)

Loft Kolasinski, loft-kolasinski.com (Marmalade Factory apartment, Szczecin, Poland)

Luchetti Krelle, luchettikrelle.com (Ovolo 1888 Darling Harbour, Sydney, Australia)

Marc Merckx Interiors, merckxinteriors.com (The Robey, Chicago, USA)

Mark Lewis Interior Design, marklewisinteriordesign.com (Hampstead home, London, UK; Hoxton Square home, London, UK)

Menu, menuspace.com (The Audo, Copenhagen, Denmark)

Morris Adjmi, ma.com (Wythe Hotel, New York City, USA)

Mostaghim, mostaghim.com.au (Veriu Broadway, Sydney, Australia)

Neri&Hu, neriandhu.com (The Waterhouse At South Bund, Shanghai, China)

Nicolas Schuybroek Architects, ns-architects.com (The Robey, Chicago, USA)

Norm Architects, normcph.com (The Audo, Copenhagen, Denmark)

OTTOTTO, ottotto.pt (GreenHouse, Porto, Portugal)

Palette Architecture, palettearch.com (The Collective Paper Factory, New York, USA)

Paper House Project, paperhouseproject.co.uk (Florida Street garment factory, London, UK)

Pedra Liquida, pedraliquida.com (Armazém Luxury Housing, Porto, Portugal)

Plum Projects, plumprojectsllc.com (Pioneer Square Loft, Seattle, USA)

Precious McBane, preciousmcbane.com (The Zetter, London, UK)

RATIO, ratiodesign.com (Ironworks Hotel Indy, Indianapolis, USA)

Roman and Williams, romanandwilliams.com (Hotel Emma, San Antonio, USA)

SheltonMindel, sheltonmindel.com (Tribeca industrial loft, New York, USA)

Sigurd Larsen, sigurdlarsen.com (Michelberger Hotel, Berlin, Germany)

Soho House, sohohouse.com (Soho House, Chicago, USA; Soho Warehouse, Los Angeles, USA; The Hoxton, Paris, France)

Space Group Architects, spacegrouparchitects.com (Spratts Factory, London, UK)

Spik Studios, spikstudios.com (The Steam Hotel, Västerås, Sweden)

Stephen Shadley Designs, stephenshadley.com (Diane Keaton's RRR House, Los Angeles, USA)

Stonehill Taylor, stonehilltaylor.com (The Eliza Jane, New Orleans, USA)

Studio Aisslinger, aisslinger.de (Michelberger Hotel, Berlin, Germany)

Studio David Thulstrup, studiodavidthulstrup.com (Vipp Chimney House, Copenhagen, Denmark)

SuperLimão, superlimao.com.br (RF Apartment, São Paulo, Brazil)

Suppose Design Office, suppose.jp (Hotel Cycle, Onomichi, Japan)

Takacs Architecture, takacsarchitecture.com (Diane Keaton's RRR House, Los Angeles, USA)

Terzo Piano, terzo-piano.com (Bathroom rendering for Fiandre Architectural Surfaces)

Tim Lewis Studio, timlewisstudio.com (Wm. Mulherin's Sons, Philadelphia, USA)

Tonkin Zulaikha Greer Architects, tzg.com.au (The Old Clare, Sydney, Australia)

Tristan Plessis Studio, tristanplessis.com (Gorgeous George, Cape Town, South Africa)

Urbane Citizen, urbane.co.za (Gorgeous George, Cape Town, South Africa)

Vector Architects, vectorarchitects.com (Yangshuo Sugar House, Guilin, China)

Warehouse Home interior design (Shoreditch show apartment, London, UK; Urban Splash show apartment, Manchester, UK)

Workstead, workstead.com (Tribeca Loft, New York, USA)

Zarch Collaboratives, zarch.com.sg (The Warehouse Hotel, Singapore)

Stockists

&Tradition, andtradition.com
17 Patterns, 17patterns.com
Amara, amara.com
Article, article.com
Barker and Stonehouse, barkerandstonehouse.co.uk
Bellerby & Co, bellerbyandco.com
Benjamin Hubert, layerdesign.com
Buster + Punch, busterandpunch.com
BY THORNAM, bythornam.com
Cairncross Martin, cairncrossmartin.com
Carl Hansen & Son, carlhansen.com
Carpe Diem, carpediembeds.com
Casper, casper.com
Castor Design, castordesign.ca
CB2, cb2.com
Chaises Nicolle, chaises-nicolle.com
Channels, channelsdesign.com
Christopher Farr, christopherfarr.com
Common Ceramics, commonceramics.com.au
Concrete LCDA, concrete-beton.com
Coral & Tusk, coralandtusk.com
Cox & Cox, coxandcox.co.uk
Crate & Barrel, crateandbarrel.com
Crittall Windows, crittall-windows.co.uk
Cultiver, cultiver.com
Dan Funderburgh, danfunderburgh.cargo.site
Darklight, darklightdesign.com
David Krynauw, davidkrynauw.com
DCW éditions, dcw-editions.fr
Design House Stockholm, designhousestockholm.com
Dinesen, dinesen.com
Dowsing & Reynolds, dowsingandreynolds.com
Drew Millward, drewmillward.portfoliobox.me
Dusen Dusen, dusendusen.com
Dyke & Dean, dykeanddean.com
Dzek, dzekdzekdzek.com
Egg Designs, eggdesigns.com
Emeco, emeco.net
Encore Reclamation, encorereclamation.co.uk
English Salvage, englishsalvage.co.uk
Evan Raney, evanraney.com
Facaro, facaro.com
Felix Lighting Specialists, felixlightingspecialists.co.uk
Ferm Living, fermliving.com
Fernando Mastrangelo, fernandomastrangelo.com
Ferroluce, ferroluce.it
Fiandre Architectural Surfaces, granitifiandre.com
Finn Juhl, finnjuhl.com
Flavor Paper, flavorpaper.com
Floor Story, floorstory.co.uk
Flos, flos.com
Foresso, foresso.co.uk
Foscarini, foscarini.com
Frette, frette.com

Fritz Hansen, fritzhansen.com
Gregor Jenkin, gregorjenkin.com
Haldane Martin, haldane.co.za
Holloways of Ludlow, hollowaysofludlow.com
House of Hackney, houseofhackney.com
Hovia, hovia.com
Hudson Valley Lighting, hvlgroup.com
Jan Kath, jan-kath.com
Jardan, jardan.com.au
Jess Design, jessdesign.com
Jieldé, jielde.com
Kast, kastconcretebasins.com
Knoll, knoll.com
Krassky, krassky.com
Kvadrat, kvadrat.dk
Larusi, larusi.com
LASSCO, lassco.co.uk
Lasvit, lasvit.com
Lawson-Fenning, lawsonfenning.com
Lee Broom, leebroom.com
LinenMe, linenme.com
Loftlight, loftlight.pl
Logan Moody, loganmoody.com
Loom Rugs, loomrugs.com
Louise Roe, louise-roe.com
Made, made.com
Magis, magisdesign.com
Majestic Showers, majesticshowers.com
Mandarin Stone, mandarinstone.com
Marta Bakowski, martabakowski.com
Materialised, materialised.com.au
Matthew Hilton, matthewhilton.com
Max Lamb, maxlamb.org
Menu, menuspace.com
Merchant & Found, merchantandfound.com
Mineheart, mineheart.com
Montana Furniture, montanafurniture.com
Moooi, moooi.com
Moroso, moroso.it
Mr Perswall, mrperswall.com
Mullan Lighting, mullanlighting.com
Muuto, muuto.com
Nick Fraser, nickfraser.co.uk
Niki Jones, niki-jones.co.uk
Northern Lights, northern-lights.co.uk
Osmo, osmouk.com
Overgaard & Dyrman, oandd.dk
OXDENMARQ, oxdenmarq.com
Parachute, parachutehome.com
Pendleton, pendleton-usa.com
People's Industrial Design Office, peoples-products.com
Pinch Design, pinchdesign.com
Poltrona Frau, poltronafrau.com
Pooky, pooky.com

Portapivot, portapivot.com
PSLab, pslab.lighting
Rakks, rakks.com
Rebel Walls, rebelwalls.com
Restoration Hardware, rh.com
Retrouvius, retrouvius.com
Robin Sprong, robinsprong.com
Rockett St George, rockettstgeorge.co.uk
Rockit Home, rockithome.co.uk
Roll & Hill, rollandhill.com
Rose Uniacke, roseuniacke.com
Rug'Society, rugsociety.eu
Savoir Beds, savoirbeds.com
Schoolhouse Electric, schoolhouse.com
Secret Linen Store, secretlinenstore.com
Seljak Brand, seljakbrand.com.au
Sherwin-Williams, sherwin-williams.com
Simon St James, simonstjames.com
Society Limonta, societylimonta.com
Sofa.com, sofa.com
Space Copenhagen, spacecph.dk
Spoonflower, spoonflower.com
Stacy Rozich, staceyrozich.com
Steel Vintage, steelvintage.com
Stellar Works, stellarworks.com
Stephanie Birdsong, stephaniekbirdsong.com
Studio Job, studio-job.com
Surface View, surfaceview.co.uk
St. Leo, stleointeriors.com
Tabitha Bargh, tabithabargh.co.uk
Ted Jefferis, tedjefferis.com
The Conran Shop, conranshop.co.uk
The Monkey Puzzle Tree, themonkeypuzzletree.com
The Rag & Bone Man, theragandboneman.co.uk
Timorous Beasties, timorousbeasties.com
Tonone, tonone.com
Toscot, toscot.it
Vacarda Design, vacardadesign.com
Vibia, vibia.com
Vipp, vipp.com
Warehouse Home, mywarehousehome.com
Weylandts, weylandts.co.za
Workstead, workstead.com
Young & Battaglia, youngbattaglia.com
Zero Lighting, zerolighting.com
Zoffany, zoffany.com

Acknowledgements

From the author / My heartfelt thanks to Warehouse Home creative director Paul Rider and deputy editor Rachel Anderson for their constant enthusiasm and dedication to the Warehouse Home brand, and to Jenny Diprose for her invaluable early design input to this book. I am so grateful to the team at Evro Publishing, particularly Eric Verdon-Roe and Mark Hughes, for their support and encouragement. This book is dedicated to my family with all of my love.

Hotel To Home: Industrial Interiors Inspired By The World's Most Original Hotels © 2021 Sophie Bush

Published in October 2021

ISBN 978-1-527226-51-7

Published by Evro Publishing, Westrow House, Holwell, Sherborne, Dorset DT9 5LF, UK

Printed and bound in Bosnia and Herzegovina by GPS Group.

A catalogue record for this book is available from the British Library.

To see other titles from Warehouse Home, visit mywarehousehome.com

With thanks / To all of the photographers and stylists whose work features in this book and to all of the hotels, architecture practices and interior design studios that so helpfully contributed their detailed information and imagery for inclusion.

Front cover / The Old Clare, Sydney, Australia, photographed by Chris Court

Half title page / Soho House Chicago, USA, photographed by Dave Burk
Title page / Gorgeous George, Cape Town, South Africa, photographed by Claus Brechenmacher and Reiner Baumann

Pages 6-7 / The Eliza Jane, New Orleans, USA, photographed by Taggart Sorensen
Pages 70-71 / The Warehouse Hotel, Singapore, courtesy of The Warehouse Hotel
Pages 146-147 / Stamba Hotel, Tbilisi, Georgia, courtesy of Stamba Hotel
Pages 206-207 / Ovolo Woolloomooloo, Sydney, Australia, photographed by Michael Wee
Pages 268-269 / Boundary London, UK, courtesy of Boundary London

Back cover /
(Top left) Hotel Emma, San Antonio, USA, photographed by Nicole Franzen
(Top right) Lampe Gras N°211-311 by DCW éditions, photographed by Marie Pierre Morel
(Bottom left) Paramount House Hotel, Sydney, Australia, photographed by Sharyn Cairns
(Bottom right) The Zetter, London, UK, photographed by Darren Chung

WAREHOUSE HOME

INTERIOR DESIGN | PROPERTY | HOMEWARE | BOOKS

mywarehousehome.com
@mywarehousehome
contact@mywarehousehome.com